W9-BTF-755

Is There Life After Housework?

Don Aslett

Writer's
Digest
Books

Cincinnati, Ohio

Dedication

We (my favorite housekeeper and I) dedicate this book to Gladys Allen, who ironed out the wrinkles and removed the cobwebs from the script.

We also give our sweeping thanks to John Preston Creer who waxed the idea of the book, to Clark Carlile who dusted away any doubts we could do it, to Ernie Garrett and Anne Montague, who mopped up the English, to Mark Browning, who polished the style and to Judith Holmes Clarke, who decorated the pages.

Is There Life After Housework? Copyright 1981 by Don Aslett. Printed and bound in the United States of America. All rights reserved. No part of this book may be reproduced in any form or by any electronic or mechanical means including information storage and retrieval systems without permission in writing from the publisher, except by a reviewer who may quote brief passages in a review. Published by Writer's Digest Books, 9933 Alliance Road, Cincinnati, Ohio 45242.

First revised edition, July 1981
   Second printing, September 1981
Second revised edition, July 1982
   Second printing, September 1982
   Third printing, December 1982

Library of Congress Cataloging in Publication Data
Aslett, Don, 1935-
      Is there life after housework?
      Includes index.
      1. House cleaning. I. Title.
TX324.A76   648'.5   81-11666
ISBN 0-89879-067-0   AACR2

Book design by Colophon.

The
Housework
Manifesto

A neat, clean, organized home is not a luxury or an option. It is an obligation—not to your house, your family, or your neighbors, but to you.

You aren't working life away to please your windows, or to satisfy your house; you are living for fulfillment: personal joy and happiness. Your home is an extension of your personality. It is a mirror to the world of what you are. The conditions within the walls of your home, immaculate or sloppy, are an admission of how you view yourself as a person. They will not only reveal your personality, and emotional and mental outlook, but will be instrumental in your motivation for personal success or failure in all you do.

The basic disciplines and principles you apply in your homemaking will, in a serene yet penetrating way, project your personal character.

You are entitled to a life of love, fulfillment, and accomplishment, but you will find these rewards almost impossible to obtain if you spend your life thrashing and wallowing in a muddle of housework.

It is your responsibility to maintain your home, but it is by no means your total destiny. Long, grinding, unrewarding hours of toil are not necessary. Within each of you is the ability to reduce the chores of housekeeping. Once this ability is applied, the long hours of drudgery will disappear. Your home and your life will assume a spirit of order. And you will experience a freedom you have never known before.

Don A. Aslett

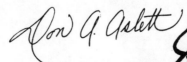

Table of Contents

Hi, I'm Neva Dunn ...
do I have a schedule, Wow!

My favorite chapters are:

You'll love them.

Hello (gasp)   I'm Dee Pleeted,

Ah'm Mae Tikulus,
ah do declare

Greetings,
Dahlinks,
I'm
Mrs.
Rollin
N. Thedoe.

When you own twenty houses
My furniture is a sight to see after
tallest chandelier is sparkling thanks to

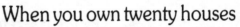

I'm Libby ... Libby Raited ... I've got limited time available
for household cleaning. But I had time for a
time management seminar after digesting
was a snap after reading

I'm Annie Septic.

Chapter 15 Shorter Visits to the Bathroom ... page 103, is copacetic.

Chapter 16 Designing Your Own Efficiency ... page 109, has helped me clean up my act.

And in **Chapter 17 What About Being a Professional Housecleaner?** ... page 113, I've found my true purpose in life.

Hi, I'm Betty Betterhouse and I felt like giving Don Aslett the old plunger ...

Until I read **Chapter 18 Your Reward: There Is Life After Housework** ... page 125

A Clean House

How Does Everyone Else Do It?

Some lie . . .

Some have mighty lumpy rugs . . .

Some have no children . . .

Some have a maid . . .

Some browbeat their husbands to do the work . . .

Some use only one room in the house . . .

Some never let anyone in . . .

Most of us don't use any of these methods to clean our houses. We represent the 95% of homemakers who, often in a state of cobweb confusion at the end of the day, wonder "How does everyone else do it?"

Every time we read or hear of another clean-and-organized success story, we end up depressed and frustrated. We try the miracle formulas, quick tips, and super systems. When we find ourselves still not progressing in the war against grime, grit, and grubbies, we again wonder why it works so well for others. "Something is surely wrong with me!" we conclude.

Psychological theory says, "A dominant reason for depression, dissatisfaction, and lack of self-esteem among American women today is their gross error in overestimating the homemaking attainments of other women." Overestimation of what other women get done is helped along by the superwoman stories we often get from television commercials and newspaper stories. The media, of course, are ever anxious to package and present any "news" the most dramatic way possible, hence even the most mundane things get romanticized! The hearer, reader, or observer can only gasp in astonishment and try to suppress that shrinking feeling of inadequacy: "Look what she's done! What's wrong with *me?*"

Slick magazines and bestselling authors have tried to provide all the answers for a "perfect home"—and have convinced too many homemakers they don't have a chance. This constant bombardment of get-clean-and-organized propaganda leaves millions of women wondering,"What's wrong with my system? Why am I the only one failing?" There is nothing wrong with you or any woman who is struggling to fulfill her responsibilities in the running of a home. Housework is, for a fact, never-ending and little appreciated. There are no superwoman homemakers. Most women are barely managing, meeting daily crises and demands, just like you are, wondering too what's wrong with them. It is amazing that for the most complicated, life-affecting job on earth, homemaking, little or no training is provided.

The superwoman articles, books, and commercials are a failure if their intent is to inspire the homemaker to rise to maximum efficiency. Gimmicks, hints, formulas, or magic schedules for "living happily ever after" are not the answer. Overestimating or underestimating your abilities in any situation feeds the monster of discouragement. When you are doing your best but see yourself falling short of your goals, it's hard to have a bright outlook or a sense of accomplishment. I assure you there are some proven methods of becoming the owner of a clean house. They don't hinge on magic, good luck, or genies in a cleaner jug. You can, by applying some professional skills, approaches, and determination, reduce your household chore time by as much as 75%. My confidence in you and in this statement is anchored in 25 years as a professional housecleaner—and teaching and listening to thousands of women across the country talk about their cleaning.

A Housecleaner Is Born

Fresh off the farm and unappreciative of my mother's labors to provide me with hearty meals, ironed shirts, and a clean bed, I found college life a far cry from a comfortable home. My appreciation for that home and mother became keener when I discovered how much it took of my time and money to support myself in the world. For survival, I landed a job bottling pop for 75¢ per hour, my first non-farm job. After deductions, the funds left were definitely not enough to get me through college. So I looked for a better-paying, part-time pastime.

Cleaning yards and houses looked like a lucrative endeavor, so my career as a world-renowned housecleaner was launched. Following afternoon classes, I would suit up in a white uniform and knock on doors asking if I could assume some of the ladies' household drudgery. I received only a few sneers before I was snatched from the street and given a furnace-cleaning job, followed later by some floors, then some windows. On every job, the women would watch and direct me, and I would scrub, shovel, and polish. Next came wallpaper cleaning, wall washing, and cupboard cleaning. Word got out that there was an eager housecleaner on the loose in the neighborhood, and soon I had more work than I needed. I hired help, taught them what the homemakers had taught me, and the business grew. Carpet and upholstery cleaning were added to my list of skills. Soon my business was a large one, in demand in towns outside the college city of Pocatello, Idaho.

In the next 10 years, into which I crowded five years of college, my unique housecleaning business received much public recognition—"College Boy Makes Good." And between newspaper headlines I acquired a vast amount of experience in housecleaning methodology. I ruined grand-piano tops, pushed over china cabinets, broke windows, streaked walls, suffocated pet birds with ammonia, ruined murals, shrank living room carpets into throw rugs, and pulled hundreds of other goofs. But with each job I got better, faster, and more efficient (at cleaning, not breaking). I cleaned log cabins with dirt floors and the plushest mansions in the country. Some days I would have five housecleaning crews in operation and would clean several three-story homes from top to bottom in less than a day.

Cleaning skills were not the only talents needed to run the company. Organization was important. All of us working in the business were full-time students, were active in church and civic affairs, and were the heads of large families.

Barbara and I had six children in seven years. While operating my business, going to school, and getting a degree, I lettered three years in college athletics and was on the debating team. Because my co-workers and I had no alternative, we *had* to develop efficient methods to clean houses. I was continually fortunate to receive much opinionated coaching and direction from every homemaker for whom I worked.

In these years of "field experience" in housecleaning and house organizing is based my confidence that I can show you how you can attain a greater level of housecleaning efficiency. Although I now serve as a consultant providing building efficiency and maintenance specifications for the world's largest companies, I know that the homemaker faces some of the most difficult problems of all—a fact not often realized or appreciated. Housework is not just housework, as most "outsiders" think. Housework is something every woman is expected to do after homemaking.

I once viewed, with a certain critical eye, my wife and other women struggling feverishly to get their housework finished. I ached to jump in and show those "disorganized gals" how an expert could square things away. Soon the opportunity, along with a great lesson, came to me. Fresh out of college, I worked hard washing walls late at night to buy my wife a surprise plane ticket to Alaska. She was delighted to have her first flight ever and a chance to see her mother again. I bade her goodbye and told her to stay as many weeks as she wished, and that I would care well for our six small children. She wasted no time leaving, I assure you. Like most men, my true thoughts were, "Now that I have her out of town, I'm really going to shape up this disorganized house and make it as efficient as my business!"

I woke up at four the first morning and confidently mapped out the campaign of great household efficiency which was about to be enacted in our home. By 6:30 the kids were up, and they saluted before they went to the bathroom! By 7:30, the beds were made and the dishes were done and I was rolling to victory. We were putting the finishing touches on a new home, and my project for the day was the construction of a vanity cabinet in the master bathroom—an easy half day's work. I had just started to glue the first board when "Waaa!" One of the kids had biffed the other. I ran out and made peace, passed out the storybooks, and again picked up the hammer and board. "Waaa!"—someone burned a finger. Three Band-Aids and 10 minutes of comforting and mercurochrome-dabbing later, I again picked up the hammer (after I scraped off the now-dry glue) and had one nail started when 'Waaa!"—a diaper to change (a cry which was repeated all day; I'd have sworn we had four in diapers at the same time). Again I returned to work, and had started the second nail, when *ding-dong* (the milkman), then *ding-dong* (the mailman), then *ring-a-ling* (the school telephoning—Laura forgot her lunch card). Then *knock-knock*—"Can I borrow. . . ." Then buzz—time for lunch ... *ding-dong* ... time for bottles. "Waaa!"—diapers again, etc., etc., etc. You would not believe how my morning went (or would you?)? My building project looked like a chimpanzee special—dried glue and badly cut boards were all over, and no real work had been accomplished. Noon came and another surprise, those little dudes don't appreciate what you do for them, all that work cooking and they threw food, slobbered, and not one of them thanked me. . . .

Nap time came, and would you believe little kids don't all go to sleep at the same time? I've bedded down 600 head of cattle easier and faster than those six kids. When I finally got them all down, no way was I going to hammer, play the stereo, or even turn a page loud and risk waking one of them! Fortunately, the day ended just before I did. I had two boards up on the cabinet by the time the last baby was read to sleep at midnight. The most famous housecleaner and best organizer in the West . . . had accomplished nothing! I was *so* tired and discouraged. The day before I'd bought seven trucks and expanded my company into a new area—but that day, nothing!

The next morning, I again woke at four and decided again I was going to run things like my business. I'd change all the diapers ahead for the whole day! But it didn't work. Leaving out all the gory details of the next few days, my half-day cabinet job, only half-complete, bit the dust. A week later my wife called to check on things. I pinched all the kids to get them howling in the background so I wouldn't have to beg her to come and save me. She did return at once, and I suddenly got efficient again.

Since this experience, my compassion, respect, and appreciation for the homemaker has grown considerably. In preparing the material for this book I have tried to keep in mind the hundreds of other jobs the homemaker must perform simultaneously. Housework *can* be shortened, and there is life after housework, but there is also life *during* housework, which must go on. Some laundry, some shopping and cooking, and some mending will always be required.

Big houses are proportionately easier to clean than small ones, new houses are easier than old, so exact methods or plans don't always work. Women trying to follow and pattern their lives after others are eventually disillusioned . . . like the determined woman who tried a simple "foolproof" formula for keeping children from getting their dirty fingerprints all over the wall. She had read a "how to run a perfect home" article which said, "Take Junior, sit him down and say, 'Junior, if you wash your hands three times a day, Mommy will give you a quarter raise in your allowance.' "

Immediately the woman called her dirty-fingered son in and presented the proposal to him. "I promise," said the son. And he kept his promise of washing his hands three times a day. But the spots were still on the wall. The mother observed her son one morning, and indeed, he was keeping the bargain. He went to the sink and washed his hands and dried them, then repeated this procedure twice more while still at the sink. Then he left to play in the dirt.

If you are offended by the gorgeous TV housewife dressed in expensive evening clothes who flips her pearl necklace out of the way to mop the floor with Magic Glow, you are not alone. I get ill watching the exaggerations of how well cleaning methods and material work when applied to a house where everything is already perfect. Occasionally a well-groomed dog ambles through the place or an immaculate kid or two tiptoes past, after which the "super-smelling clean-all," applied effortlessly, takes over. Don't be discouraged while you watch. Something is wrong with them, not you!

Miracle formulas, tricks, gimmicks, and solutions aren't the answer, and if they haven't worked for you, don't let it bother you, because the key to freedom from housework isn't there. The first principle of effective housework is not to have to do it! Being able to do it well is great, but it's greater not to have to do it at all. Your real goal is to *eliminate* all of it you can. In this book I'll show you how to get rid of a bunch of it, and the rest I'll show you how to take care of quickly and efficiently.

Household "hints" won't do it for you, but you can do it for yourself. The housewife who does housework "just to get it done" is like the teacher who wades through one confused, disorderly, unmotivated class after the other waiting to be saved by the bell. Getting "finished" with any housework chore is a worthwhile goal, but doing it in teeth-gritting agony is self-defeating. There are "have-to" jobs, no matter how good we are (bathroom rings, fingerprints). You'll never escape them. However, when you learn to minimize the time you spend on the have-to jobs, you'll finally be able to get to the "get-to jobs" and they'll both become more pleasant, I promise! There *is* life after housework—and if you do it right, there can be life *during* housework.

Once you start finding the extra time that once was all spent on housework, nothing in your home will be mediocre or dull. You'll rip down anything that is faded or ugly and replace it with the prettiest, the most colorful, most refreshing things you can find or make. You'll throw out or trade things that don't fit in. If something is torn or worn or forlorn, you'll look forward to taking care of it, not as a chore, but as a chance to better yourself or others. You'll want to mend it, because it will be mending *you*. Once you have time, you'll be inspired to repair it if it sags, refinish it if it's dull. The real struggle before was not in the chore or item you had to service, it was the hopeless feeling that there was never any time for it. A lot of "little" things that need to be done really aren't work once you can get to them—and once you really believe that you can, you'll start looking forward to them! That's life *during* housework!

At the housecleaning seminars I've taught across the country, I've passed out thousands and thousands of registration cards with a space left for comments, special requests, or housecleaning wisdom. This was written on one (can you detect a worry this person might have that you don't?): "I must tell you, I love to clean. I have a clean house and I've been using the same techniques you use for years now. Everything in my house looks good, but my husband accuses me of being lazy because I don't exhaust myself every day like his mother did. I make lots of handicrafts and pillows and things, and he can't get over the fact that everything is clean and yet I still have time to goof off. He is honestly upset. He thinks I don't work enough and have too much fun."

You can't win 'em all. You'll discover in your worrying about how other people do it that 90% of the time you are overestimating their results. Even in the cartoon world, Superwoman in all her glory never raised children, stabilized a husband, or cleaned and managed a house. Superwoman faced only criminals, not housework horrors. You can be as much a superwoman as anyone you'll meet or read about, if you will only learn to harness your own resources. Not many others are more efficient or have a neater house than you.

By following the simple secrets in this book, you'll become even more efficient, and will have more time to enjoy life after housework.

The Old Wives' Tales...

2

Ever Hear These?

"I paint every year. It's cheaper than cleaning."

"Never shampoo carpets when they're new; they get dirty faster."

"Spring is the time to clean."

"Toothpaste and peanut butter remove black marks."

"Start washing from the bottom of the wall and work up."

"Always clean one room at a time."

"Newspapers are the best polishing material."

"Dried bread crumbs clean wallpaper."

Some of these might possibly work, but why go the long way around to get the job done? Spring is not the best time to clean a house inside, late fall is. Who wants to be cooped up with paint and ammonia fumes, when springtime blossoms are fragrant? Painting isn't cheaper than cleaning; cleaning averages 60 to 70% less. Carpets don't get dirty faster after the first shampooing, if you do it right, and newspapers are not good for polishing (only for training puppies and peeks at the funnies). Toothpaste and peanut butter remove marks because they are abrasive, but they also cut the gloss of good enamel paint, and the resulting dull patch looks worse than the original mark.

For centuries, "secrets" of sure-cleaning brews have been passed on to young housekeepers. These formulas are tried unsuccessfully and on deathbeds are whispered to the next generation. Hence, even in this day of modern science, well-educated homemakers living in modern homes are still using dried frogs' legs to remove inkstains in their carpets and vinegar-soaked cottage cheese to polish brass doorknobs.

I have yet to find a magic cleaner or solution that will do all the work in cleaning a house. Less than 2% of the old wives' tales whispered to me by hundreds of women ever worked. And there is no magic in the bottle, either. The "cleaning cyclone" that whips out of the container isn't interested in cleaning for you when it is getting $150,000 for a minute on TV. Even if that solution—or any solution—

is as good as advertisers say it is, it will have little effect on your cleaning time.

Forget most of the old wives' tales and commercials that you have heard and follow some of the simple professional methods that have been used efficiently and safely for decades.

Whatever you do, don't feel it your economic duty to mix up your own money-saving brew. Some of the results are ridiculous. For example, it's easy to make your own glue, isn't it? Just·find an old cow, kill it, and cut off as many hooves as you need for as much glue as you want. Grind them up in your trusty blender, then add. . . . It's not worth it when you can spend 39¢ and get something better. Besides, it's cheaper than finding a cow and not nearly as messy as killing one. Women trying to make their own home-brew furniture polish will spend three hours of their time rounding up the materials and mixing up a solution that

costs $5.45 for ingredients alone instead of buying a commercial polish for $2.49 which is tested, safe, and guaranteed not to rot, explode, or poison. Remember, it is your *time* that is valuable. A half century of professional cleaners' records show that out of every dollar spent for cleaning, only 8¢ is for supplies and equipment, and almost the same ratio holds true in the home. Your time and safety are the valuable commodities, not the supplies. Don't spend your precious hours grinding and rubbing trying to get vinegar to perform like soap. Vinegar is not a cleaner, it's a rinsing agent. The "squeak" is what turns you on!

Figuring this from a "free me from housework" angle, it means that using good, efficient, and even expensive supplies and equipment is a cheap way to go if it cuts your time down. For example, if you pay $50 for a gallon of wax, it is a good buy if its quality is such that whatever you apply it to requires only annual or biennial cleaning and waxing.

What's a woman to do? If you can read, you can forget the "witch potions" and the glamorously packaged, overpriced "household cleaners" you've been using. The Yellow Pages in almost every phone directory in the world lists "janitorial supplies" firms. These are (generally) wholesale outlets where commercial cleaning companies buy many of their supplies. (This is where to find the items I refer to in this book and that can't be bought at the supermarket or hardware store.) The rest they buy at the local supermarket, same as you do. The prices at a janitorial supply house vary with the policy, but I've never run into one in the multi-state area where I have cleaned that would not sell to a homemaker.

Wholesale or retail? Well, you can get either price. The best way to try for wholesale price is to walk in with dignity and authority, squinting confidently at the shelves of cleaning material and equipment (few of which you'll recognize the first time) and say, "I'm

Mrs. Van Snoot of Snoot and Snoot, Frisky, and Melvin (you, your husband, cat, and dog). I need one gallon of metal interlock self-polishing floor finish." This usually convinces the seller that you are official, and he will generally treat you right, offering you a contractor's price, since most suppliers are great people and run "hungry" establishments. If they ask you a question such as, "Do you want polymer or carnauba base?" don't lose your nerve. Just say, "Give me the house's best-selling brand." (Forty janitor companies can't be wrong!) I'm sure if you don't get the contractor's price, you will get a discount.

A woman's household tools are her power tools. A gross injustice is usually inflicted on women in this area. Over and over, I see situations where women are using an old rattletrap vacuum hardly capable of running, let alone sucking up any dirt. The hose is full of holes, the cord is worn and offers instant electrocution if touched in the wrong place. Every day wives wrestle with these machines to do the housework, while in the basement or garage sits a $400 radial-arm saw or other power tool which the husband doesn't use or hasn't used in six months! The man needs these macho tools to give his masculinity an occasional boost—while the woman fights an unsafe, ineffective vacuum for hours . . . every day! Husbands' closets are full of expensive guns which the men use one or two days a year, while their wives are cooking three square meals on an electric stove with worn-out switches, or bunching tricot on a 20-year-old single-stitch sewing machine . . . daily! Even the woman's junk drawer (you know, that drawer with all the parts, spare tools, lids, screws, handles, matches, nails, etc.) is used more by the man than the drawer in his $800 solid oak workbench.

In most cases, after an industrious proj-

ect or two, men seldom use their expensive tools; as investments go, such tools are poor ones. A woman's time is her most valuable commodity, and good housecleaning tools and equipment can save hundreds of hours a year. Husbands and wives should take a serious look around their houses. The tools likely to be used most and those capable of saving the most time are the ones that should be purchased. Avoid "trinket" attachments to cleaning machines or appliances of any kind. Stick to solid tools and supplies.

Which Supplies to Use: Where and When?

I will outline these as we cover each area of cleaning. Just remember this: There is no magic in the bottle or machine. The basics of effective cleaning are extremely simple. I have listed on the chart at the end of this chapter the basic "professional tools" which you will find useful. I would consider a home well prepared for cleaning and maintaining efficiently if equipped with the items that appear there.

Proper Supplies—Big Returns

There are more benefits from using the right equipment and supplies than merely doing a (1) faster and (2) better job. There are: (3) safety—you will be using fewer, simpler items that will be safer for you and children to use and store; (4) cost—you will spend 75% less money on cleaning supplies if you select and use them properly; (5) depreciation—using proper cleaning supplies and tools reduces damage and deterioration of the surfaces and structures you're cleaning; (6) storage—few apartments, mobile homes, or, for that matter, houses—have enough storage space.

If your cleaning closet is full of fancy cans and bottles—Zippo, Rippo, Snort, Rubb Off, Scale Off, Goof Off—I promise a roomier closet when you learn the secrets of proper cleaning. Many of those chemicals and cleaners crammed into every cupboard and under every sink are not that effective for cleaning. They are safety hazards for children. Many are damaging to household surfaces and they all take up valuable storage room.

Canned expense: The aerosol can has pressured itself into the lives of all. Toothpaste, hairspray, kettle grease—just about everything comes in aerosol because we've been convinced it takes too much effort to do any more than push a button. We have carried this principle over into our housecleaning systems, paying dollars for pennies' worth of cleaners and compressed gas. Some aerosols are convenient enough to justify buying them, but for the most part, you don't get your money's worth in mileage or quality. To replace most of the aerosols you use, go to the janitorial house and buy four or five reusable commercial plastic spray bottles. Buy your chemicals, cleaners, and disinfectants concentrated, in gallons. Mix them with water at the suggested dilution ratios and put the solutions in the spray bottles. Label the bottles with a waterproof pen or make sure each chemical is a different color, lest you end up cleaning windows with upholstery shampoo. These plastic spray bottles are unbreakable, durable, won't nick cupboards, and are extremely efficient and economical to use.

When using any kind of cleaner, commercial or household, *read the label*. Don't sniff to see what's in the jug; a rose will never smell the same if you ever get a strong whiff from a commercial ammonia bottle. And be sure to dilute cleaners properly. Our tendency is to say, "If a little does a good job, a lot will do better." This is as erroneous as saying, "if a teaspoon of salt or baking powder will help the biscuits, then a cup of each will help them a lot more." We often gluggy-glug-glug too much soap in the water and actually destroy the suspension and cutting action of the chemical. Read the directions before pouring. Remember, you don't clean alone. You have two helpers, water and chemicals; they will do most of the work.

"Miracle" solutions and "magic" tools aren't the only carry-over from old wives' tales. Household advice columns are everywhere in newspapers and magazines. "Helpful hints" often only help add frustration. Out of a recent "40 Ways to Save Time in the Home" article, I found only one tip that was beneficial. Many of them if applied to my operation would result in chaos and bankruptcy. Be discerning, check sources, and use your head in choosing housecleaning "advice."

You can get by without the kind of advice that always says things like "buy a second vacuum cleaner for upstairs" and "color-coordinate all your bathrooms so the towels will match anywhere and things will be pretty for unexpected company." What you need to learn most of all is how to choose and use supplies and materials so as to use fewer

Caution

Read the label—Don't sniff to see what it is!

hours of your time to do better quality housecleaning. I will explain how to accomplish this as we cover each major cleaning area in detail.

Now . . . to dispel one last and most famous old *husband's* tale: the value of a woman's time. On this earth, no one's time is worth any more than anyone else's. I used to send my wife to town or on errands to do "the piddly things" because my time was worth "so much"—after all, I could get $50 to $100 an hour for consulting jobs. I was way off base. *Any woman's time is worth what any man's is.*

Time, calculated in terms of the ability to appreciate, to feel, to love, to experience, is of equal value to all human beings. Pay per hour or position doesn't dictate how much a person's time is worth. Anything that can be purchased to save time in housework is just as important as a new computer for the business! Buy up!

By the way—did you know that a paste of strawberries and wheat germ, ground glass, and baking soda will polish the bottom of a Boy Scout's cooking kit? (But so will a 2¢ scouring pad!)

EQUIPMENT AND SUPPLIES CHART

Here's a chart illustrating some of the basic professional tools, equipment, and supplies that m
housekeeping faster and easier. Most of these items can be found at a Janitorial Supply hous

ITEM	TYPE/SIZE	USE
SQUEEGEE	10", 12", or 14" brass—Ettore Steccone is a good brand.	Strictly for window cleaning, avoid contact with rough surfaces to keep rubber blade perfectly sharp. (Fits on Extension Handle.)
GOLDEN GLOVE	10" or 12" aluminum holder with fabric head.	Use to apply cleaning solution to windows prior to squeegeeing. Also great for high dusting. (Fits on Extension Handle.)
DELUXE EXTENSION HANDLE	4'–8' Metal with rubber handle.	Lightweight and easy to use. Extends from 4' to 8' to safely and accurately reach high places. (Fits squeegee and brushes.)
DRY SPONGE	5" x 7" x ½" Chemically treated natural rubber.	(Don's favorite housecleaning tool.) Use on flat wall and ceiling surfaces and wallpaper. Discard when black or soiled. Cleans many surfaces better than liquid cleans. Nonmessy and *fast!*
SCRUBEE DOODLE DOO	5" x 10" hand tool with nylon pad.	That great hand floor scrubber. To scrub edges of hard surface floors. Don wouldn't trade his for a $120.00 floor machine. (The holder comes prepacked with 3 pads.)
CLEANING CLOTH	9" by 18" doubled cotton terry cloth. (See instructions in text for making your own.)	Replaces the "rag." Used for all cleaning jobs; especially effective in wall and ceiling cleaning. Fold and turn inside out for 16 cleaning surfaces.
BOWL CADDY AND SWAB	3" cotton heavy-duty bowl swab.	To use bowl cleaner neatly and safely. Swab is used to force water out of toilet bowl (see page 106) and to lightly swab the interior of the toilet bowl with bowl cleaner.
SCRUBBING SPONGE	3" x 6" x ¾" two-layer white nylon.	Use where limited abrasion is needed. On fixtures, sinks, shower, etc. Always wet before using. Squeeze —don't wring. Good in the bathroom.
SPRAY BOTTLE	1 quart commercial plastic, trigger spray.	To fill with diluted concentrates for hand spray work on spots, bathroom, windows, and any small cleaning duty. Several of these around the house are a good investment.
MASSLIN CLOTH	11" x 17" treated paper.	For dusting; the specially treated "cloth" collects dust instead of scattering it. Disposable. Prevents gunk build-up.

ITEM	TYPE/SIZE	USE
RAINBOW DUSTER	Synthetic lamb's wool on a 24″ handle.	We've used these commercially for years. They are even better in homes for high dusting, picture frames, moldings, cobwebs, etc.
DUST MOP	16″ or 18″ cotton with rotating handle.	For use on all hard floors. Fast and efficient; lasts for years. Treat occasionally with dust mop treatment. 1 can will last 6 years. Launder and re-treat when dirt-saturated.
MATS (Indoor and Outdoor)	3′ x 4′, 3′ x 5′, or 3′ x 6′ — nylon or olefin fiber on vinyl or rubber backing.	Help to remove dust, grit and other debris from shoes and clothing, absorb mud and water from foot traffic. Available in a range of colors.
DISINFECTANT CLEANER	Concentrate — gallon, quart, or packet size.	Dilute with water for use in bathroom cleaning or mopping wherever sanitation is essential. It is a neutral cleaner and can be used for general household jobs. (Dilute as per directions.)
NEUTRAL CLEANER	Concentrate — gallon, quart, or packet size.	For mopping, spray-cleaning, paintwork, paneling, and all general cleaning where a disinfectant is not needed. Also for removing fingermarks from furniture. (Dilute as per directions.)
WET/DRY VACUUM	5 gallon metal or plastic tank.	Use this for all household vacuuming, to pick up water when scrubbing floor; for overflows, spills. Get squeegee, upholstery, and edge-tool attachments with it.
PUMICE STONE	1″ x 4″ bar.	For easy removal of toilet bowl rings; safe, lasts years.
UPRIGHT VACUUM	12″ 6 amp commercial model with cloth bag.	Basically for carpet and rug vacuuming. Don't buy half a dozen attachments; get a long cord.

For your convenience, these items are available by mail. For more information and a free catalog write to: HOUSEWORK, P.O. Box 1682, Pocatello, ID 83204

The basic janitorial cleaning compounds described in this chart and elsewhere in this book are no less dangerous than many of the cleaning preparations found on supermarket shelves. But since most janitorial supplies do not come with child-proof lids, be sure to keep them out of the reach of small children.

Is It Organization or Your Energy Level . . .

3

"I get the feeling at the end of every day that I haven't gotten anywhere and I'm not ever getting anywhere . . ." This was the comment of a beautiful blond mother with a brand-new house and four small children. She rather concisely summed up a basic problem concerning homemaking efficiency and accomplishment. Understanding your responsibility but feeling that you lack the skill or direction to fulfill it often creates total discouragement. Even if you know what the rewards of total effort will be, constantly thinking you aren't getting there will begin to prevent you from *wanting* to get there.

The Big Magic Word

The sacred, magic word to homemakers, business managers—in fact, all of us—is *organization*. If we could organize ourselves correctly, we could do anything (so we think). We spend a great deal of time trying to organize ourselves like the superwoman and superman formulas say we should, but still seem to get little accomplished. We subconsciously figure the "organizing" is going to do it for us. This is wrong. There is no "organization" that gives the answer or does the work. Is there hope? Yes, and this bit of good news will start this chapter off right—women are better organizers than men. I say so, and if you ask any boss, school principal, minister, leader, who organizes best, they will agree with me: *women do!*

There is no one best way to organize. Organization is an ever-changing process; it's a journey, not a destination. Every minute of every day a new approach is being thought up. Everyone is different in makeup, energy, concept of reality, principles, proportions, race, or origin; every situation requires a different style of organization to get the job done. The secret isn't in getting organized—it's in wanting to get the job done and committing oneself to do it. Once that is achieved, everything will fall into place. You can organize as well as anyone if you want to or have to. There isn't any "set" way to do anything. You don't have to eat dessert after a meal—you can eat it before. Your system of organization should fit you personally. It should be patterned and tailored to fit your style, your energy, your schedule, and your motivation. You run your own life—the clock doesn't run it.

Some organizational myths. I'm convinced that everyone can be organized if she has to be and if she will quit trying to follow "know-it-all" methods and formulas for keeping a perfect house. For example, the efficiency experts give a foolproof method of attaining great accomplishments. They say, in essence, "Sit yourself down and make a list of the things you want to accomplish. Put the most important ones first. When you get up in the morning, start on the first one and do not leave it or go to the next one until the first one is finished. Then go on to the second one and likewise until you are finished with the list." I can't imagine anyone being able to exist (let alone succeed) following that kind of organizational concept. It is grossly inefficient, noncreative, inflexible—not to mention no fun. I know many housewives who have been trying desperately to organize their lives and housework to fit this ridiculous concept, and they are paying dearly for it. They suffer endless frustrations because they can't make it work for them. If I followed that style of organization in my business or personal activities, I'd be 20 years behind!

Look where trying to follow the 1-2-3-4 style of getting things done would lead you. Let's say you make a list of the following things to do this week (in addition to your regular chores):

1. Make the kids a birdhouse.
2. Water the garden.
3. Memorize your part of the poem for the PTA play.
4. Send Grandmother a birthday card.
5. Get the new lawn in.

Enthusiastically, you tackle the five projects in the down-the-list style outlined by the efficiency experts. While in town, you pick up the birdhouse materials, and soon you get started on the house with full gusto; however, you forgot to get an adjustable bit to make a hole in the front of the birdhouse. So, at a critical point, you are stopped. The 1-2-3 track compels you to leave the task and take time out to secure the needed tool, which you do at a cost of six miles of driving and two hours of searching. You then paint an undercoat on the birdhouse, wait a day for it to dry, and then the second coat goes on. After two days, task #1 is at last finished, so out to the garden next. You turn on the water. Four hours later the water is finally down the rows and task #2 is finished. Next you go into the house for a few hours to memorize the PTA poem, #3 on the list. Grandmother's card, item #4, is then picked up at the store, brought home, signed and addressed, then taken to the post office. To put a hero's touch on #5, you pick up a book on lawns, work on the lawn for the last three days, and are finished with all your projects in one week!

Efficiency experts might have a week to spend to do all this, but you don't and neither do I. The tasks could easily be done in a day or more, of course, with a little daydreaming time on the side. How? By relying on your own creativity and a more flexible system. While in town, before anything is started, pick up the card for Grandmother. While driving on to get the birdhouse materials, mentally build the house so that you'll be aware of each thing that has to be picked up. While waiting for the lumberyard clerk to round up the materials, chat with one of the staff about lawn season and grass and at this time get the fertilizer, mulch, and seed for the anticipated lawn.

On the way home, turn off the car radio and start to memorize the PTA poem. Once you get home, lay out the materials for the birdhouse and build it. (Oops, we forgot the adjustable bit, too.) Let's stop the birdhouse immediately and go turn the water on for the garden, taking the poem with us to memorize while waiting for the water to get down the rows. Once the water is going, planting the lawn gets attention. Next, phone the neighbor asking him to send his adjustable bit for the birdhouse home with your child who is coming by in a while from school. Continue to work on the lawn until you are too tired to hustle. After washing for supper, sign Grandmother's card so the children can take it to the mailbox on their way to school. When your child arrives with the adjustable bit, drill the hole and paint the birdhouse. By this time, you are rested, so you tackle the lawn again. When tired, but finished, you come in and give the birdhouse a second coat. By then it's late, but just time for another shot at the poem, and you've memorized it. Now all five things are completed *in one day* instead of a week, and look at the time you have left for yourself.

Impossible to do all that in one day? No. And you can apply this same principle to housework if you rely on your own skills and really want to get it done. Your freedom and ingenuity will produce creative energy. It's simply a matter of "multiple track" organization. In housework, if you wait until one thing is completed before you start another, you'll take forever to finish and never get around to any freedom to enjoy life. Once you train yourself to the multiple-track system, thinking will be effortless. You'll just roll along accomplishing things. You won't have to drain your think tank or worry or sweat to organize. It will come naturally.

Here is the secret: The start and finish of a job are the difficult parts. So start the first project at once! As it gets rolling, begin the second. As the second gets in gear, attack the third.

By then the second one is done, so pounce on the fourth, fifth, and sixth, and if the third isn't done, start on the seventh. Don't start and finish any two tasks at the same time. Don't start one thing when you are finishing another. Start another project while you are in the middle of three or four, but don't start one at the end of another project. The multiple-track system is the correct way to run many projects at the same time. It's easy if you alternate starting and finishing times.

The way some women cook is a prime example of doing things the most efficient way. I've watched my grandmother, who had 15 children, prepare eight different dishes for 12 people in just minutes—a miracle. But it isn't a miracle, it's just good organization and the multiple-track system. She simply got eight things going at alternate times, nothing starting or ending at the same time. You've done that, haven't you, when you had to? No sense waiting for water to boil, biscuits to rise, salads to cool, lard to melt. She simply used the waiting time productively.

I've watched a one-track-mind mother with one small child crumple in total frustration trying to manage her baby. Five years, a couple of sets of twins and two singles later, she is doing a marvelous job. How? She learned the four- or five-track organization system and applied it! Your mind is capable of it and your body is, too. The success of this system is amazingly exhilarating, and once you get it down, you'll use it beneficially in every area of your life.

A large percentage of our housecleaning time is spent "putting out brush fires," as it's called in the professional field. This simply means if you would take three seconds to close the door or gate behind you, you wouldn't have to spend three days hunting for your dog. Many a housekeeper fails because all her efforts are spent taking care of problems that a little timely action would have prevented.

Homemakers are notorious for this. They will spend 20 hours a year (and a lot of mental anguish) trying to remove felt-tip marker writing from walls, instead of a minute putting the pens out of reach of the kids; 10 hours a year cleaning ovens or stove tops instead of 15 minutes choosing and preparing a container that won't boil or slop over!

Simplicity vs. Procrastination

A great deal of effort is expended as a result of failures to put out a simple timely effort. Here is a common everyday example: doing the dishes later instead of right after the meal. Notice how a simple chore multiplies itself into an insurmountable obstacle of negative results and freedom-robbing discouragement. Do you take the time, over and over, to cope with an unsatisfactory situation instead of correcting the underlying problem, like trying to adjust the faucet handle just right so the drip is minimized, angling and massaging that sticky drawer for 30 seconds every time you use it so it will slide back in, wondering and experimenting every time a fuse

HOW HOUSEWORK MULTIPLIES
HOW HOUSEWORK MULTIPLIES
HOW HOUSEWORK MULTIPLIES
HOW HOUSEWORK MULTIPLIES

If you let the dishes wait instead of doing them right after the meal:

Takes longer	Food gets harder and harder to remove. Uses more soap and water. Uses more energy. Greater breakage potential. Fewer volunteers.
Unhealthy	Bacteria have a chance to breed. Unpleasant odor. Attracts flies, roaches, and pets.
Unsightly appearance	Every glance discourages. Lowers your self-esteem. Friends gossip.
Irritates family	Members of family complain. You can't find a clean glass in the house.

blows—which breaker switch is the lights, which is the heater, which is the outlet, which is the. . . . I think you know what I mean.

The best "organization" is simply making a choice of when and how you are going to do things before they get out of hand and dictate to you how and when they will be done. Are you the slave or the master? Simplicity seldom goes hand in hand with procrastination. Do you clean up and put away things as soon as you are through (simplicity), or do you throw them in a "clean" pile to be rummaged through as they are needed (procrastination)? It only takes a few minutes to iron a blouse. Do you do it before it is needed, or five tense minutes before you have to dash out the

**Miscellaneous
Time-Savers**

**Fix those items that
always slow you up.**

door? Do you make your bed when you jump out (simplicity) or just before you go to bed again at night (procrastination)?

Do you fill out that speakers committee report when it's still fresh in your mind and will take only a few minutes; or do it when it's overdue? You've been strongly reminded to get it in, and now you'll spend hours, because now you've forgotten facts, mislaid evidence, have to write an excuse letter, etc.

The time between doing most things now and later compounds and multiplies

problems. You end up spending time not simply getting the job done, but fighting and recovering from the problems created because you waited. Doing things when they take less time is not only good scheduling, it makes good sense, and will save enough energy and motivation to apply to more personally satisfying efforts than housework.

The Ever-Famous List.

Lists are great. We all have our lists of things to do. I'd be lost without mine! We don't always do the things on the list, but they are always jotted down. At one time, my list spiraled to 76 "immediate" things to be done. It soon started taking all my time just to transfer the list to a new piece of paper when the old one wore out. If your list follows the typical pattern, at the bottom are the hard, unpleasant things, such as:

38. Tell Jack he's to be terminated.

39. Pour concrete on the back step.

40. Go face the banker and get the loan.

41. Get my wisdom teeth pulled.

42. Speak to George about taking a few more baths.

or

19. Clean the oven.

20. Clean the three-section storm windows.

21. Volunteer to tend Dennis the Menace.

22. Kick cousin Jack out of the front room.

23. Go through 700 old issues of *Good Housekeeping*.

We have to be careful with that villain list. We are often so proud of ourselves for even writing something down on our list of things to be done, we immediately relax. We say to ourselves, "Boy, I'm glad I got that one started." After a few days we suddenly realize that nothing has been done, and we sneak a look at the list to see if that item has disappeared. It hasn't. We are so relieved to know that it wasn't forgotten, we leave it for a few more days. The day before the deadline, we have to face it, and generally we get the item done in half the time we feared it would take!

A list has one big value and that is getting things itemized and recorded before you forget them. That's all! As for using a list to discipline yourself, forget it. You have to *do* the things—the list will not do them for you. I dislike the regimentation of set schedules and believe they are only for inefficient people who are afraid they are going to run out of things to do. Some budgeting of time and some scheduling is needed, but not to the extent that it dictates your *every* move and mood. You should run a schedule for your benefit, not the reverse. It can't be illustrated better than by a skit sent to me by homemaker Gladys Allen:

(Aslett arrives at the highly polished door of Mrs. Polly Programmed.)

Polly: (Wearing a huge watch on her arm, feather duster in hand. She's groomed and dressed immaculately.) Hi, Mr. Aslett, won't you please take off your shoes and come in. (Dusts him off lightly as he removes his shoes.) How nice to have a visitor drop by. I have 6¼ minutes' relaxation time (checking her watch) before I have to knead the bread and water the alfalfa sprouts.

Aslett: Mrs. Programmed, I see that you're busy. . . . I just stopped by to invite you to a little efficiency seminar.

Polly: Nonsense! Now you come right here and sit down. I still have 5 minutes and 33 seconds of leisure time.

Aslett: (Sits down) As you know, Mrs. P. . . .

Polly: (Interrupting) Oh, Mr. Aslett, would you mind sitting on this cushion? That one has already been sat on this morning. I like to alternate. The fabric wears much longer that way.

Aslett: (Moving to another cushion) Really? Now, I never would have thought of that.

Polly: My, yes! My last divan lasted 78 days longer just by using that one little trick.

Aslett: What I've come to tell you, Mrs. Programmed, is that I've come up with a great new idea for a housecleaning seminar, and I'd like to invite you to come preview it tomorrow morning at ten o'clock.

Polly: Ten o'clock Thursday? (Rushes to a big box labeled "Daily Schedules.") I've just typed up my schedules for the month. I'll have to check. (Pulls out a long folded sheet.)

Aslett: Is that your schedule for just one month?

Polly: One month? Oh, my, no! This is my schedule for Thursday. (Studies it carefully, consults watch, makes a few changes with a pencil.) Now, what time did you say that would start tomorrow?

Aslett: 10:00 a.m.

Polly: (Making a few more changes) Yes, yes, I think I'll be able to work it in after all. If I get up at 5:00 a.m. instead of 6:00, I can have my laundry sorted and my scripture studies done by 7:00. I can get my drapes vacuumed and my children fed by 7:47. While they practice their violins, I can shine the furniture and wash the dishes. They leave for school at 8:19, which gives me just enough time to stir up a casserole for supper and get myself ready. Umm, yes. I should be able to leave here by 9:37 at the latest. By the way, Mr. Aslett, what did you say your seminar will be about?

Aslett: (Stands up with a sigh, shrugs weakly, unable to speak.)

Highs and Lows

The old up-and-down pattern is entrenched in our style of living. How devastating it is to human feelings *and* efficient housekeeping. "Top of the world one day and bottom of the barrel the next" has been eased into an expected high weekend and blue Monday. Most housecleaners unthinkingly roll along with this style. We clean the house, water the plants, and do everything just so and we are "up." Immediately the condition of spotlessness and satisfaction we have attained begins to erode as dust, spiders, children, animals, husband, and guests mount their attack. It's so frustrating, since we've expended so much dedication and energy getting the house to its previous peak.

One elderly gentleman, recalling his mother's approach to housework, said, "She organized herself and family so that all the housework (washing, ironing, baking, sewing, etc.) was done on Monday (one day, mind you). What an accomplishment. But she spent the other six days recovering to prepare for the big Monday cleanup again."

This kind of housecleaning approach gets old fast, and it gets you nowhere except an early grave. Even if your house is clean as often as it is dirty (50-50), you'll not be rewarded 50-50, because it's human nature to notice and respond to the negative, not the positive. Very little is heard about the house if it's clean, but if it's dirty, everybody squawks, gossips, and complains. It's demoralizing, but you can't give up the battle. So you buckle down and restore your domain to order and cleanliness. Now hold it. Now that you've got your house in top shape again, try something different.

A little *consistency* reduces the need for

expending a lot of time, energy, and discouragement. Avoid the "up and down" style of housekeeping. Establish an *acceptable* cleanliness level and maintain it daily. If you really want to be freed from housework drudgery, this one change in style will work wonders for you. When you learn to keep house on a straight line, you'll not only find extra hours appearing, but some of the other up-and-down styles you've been struggling with for years (diets, meals, letter writing, PTA assignments, etc.) will follow your housecleaning system and suddenly begin to be manageable. Your home will never stay static. It will be in a constant state of flux, if it is used as all homes should be. Avoid extremes both ways—too much polish is just as off-putting as too little. Gold-plating a house won't return you anything but discouragement and worry.

Remember to tie scheduling and organization to your own personal motivation or energy level. Add to that the conviction that what you have to do or want to do is really worth it, and organization will fall into place. You are a human being, not a machine. You don't start running at full efficiency the minute you're cranked up. If you try it, you are going to end up mighty discouraged. Don't work for a list or a schedule—fit everything to your emotional, physical, or mental state. By tying my energy level to production, I can knock out three magazine articles in an hour; I can't do one in eight hours when I have the drags. When I'm rolling, I tackle my most active and demanding work. When the drags invade, I file, sort, or do something that requires no creativity or mental energy. In both situations, I am accomplishing a lot—I'm fitting the task to my mood and my personality. Be yourself and decide what is most important to you. Wade into it during your best hours for that particular chore, and a miracle will happen. (You might end up writing an organization book and selling it back to the superwomen of the world.)

Right now, I feel like writing Chapter 4.

4

Treasure Sorting and Storage Strategy

While cleaning a large, plush home during my junior year in college, I managed to wade through and clean an expensive, treasure-laden bedroom and embarked on cleaning the closet. In addition to the expected wardrobe of expensive wearing apparel, I had to move five exquisite cigarette lighters, 47 pairs of women's shoes (I kid you not), a case of 1916 *National Geographics,* several tennis racquets, 14 boxes of Christmas cards, six poodle collars, and numerous other items. It was a full but neat closet which was in harmony with the style of the lady who lived there. She was 55 years old. She pos-

sessed a fine home decorated with elaborate art and delicate tapestries which she had spent part of her life collecting and the rest of her life cleaning and keeping track of. For 35 years, she had managed to keep her house clean and organized and all of her things dusted. This project of shuffling treasures around had taken her a lifetime.

Most of us are in the same condition as this owner of 47 pairs of shoes. Our treasures may not be expensive, but we have as many of them crammed in as many cubbyholes which we shuffle through, sort and re-sort, climb over, worry about, and maintain for hours on end. What does it contribute to our personal edification or lifestyle? Seventy percent of it can simply and accurately be labeled JUNK. JUNK has frustrated more women than Robert Redford or Burt Reynolds. JUNK has burned down more homes, caused more ulcers, and resulted in more arguments than can be imagined. In the meantime, shuffling and dodging around it continues to take a considerable toll of our personal freedom.

All for what reason? Accumulation? Sentiment? Security? Who knows?

The other 30% of the "things" that we have lying, kicking, and stored around are of some worth to us. Small, important items left over from sewing, plumbing, playing or a thousand other pastimes or projects can, at the right moment, be worth a hundred times their value. But remember, we're talking about 30% of what we have. Why own a houseful of useless objects that rob you of time and energy?

The Burden of Junk

It is amazing how we get ourselves into the junk habit. As the Law of the Packrat goes, "Junk will accumulate proportionately to the storage room available for it."

Before learning the shortcuts and professional methods of cleaning a house, we must first learn the art of "treasure sorting." This means differentiating between valuable junk and useless junk and promptly disposing of the latter. It is a job that you cannot palm off on anyone else, or postpone too long, because there is no escape from the toll that junk takes of your life. Everything stashed away or hidden discreetly or indiscreetly is also stashed away in your mind and is subconsciously draining your mental energy. Once discarded, it is discarded from your mind, and you are free from keeping mental tabs on it. Second homes often do this to people who can afford them. The owners maintain them mentally and physically for the complete year

and use them for a couple of weeks. If it were possible to calculate the emotions and affections, the caring and sharing energy that is silently burned up worrying about the home, it would surely outweigh the benefits of a couple of weeks or months occupying the dwelling.

Another burden junk thrusts on us is that we feel obligated to use it whether we need it or not. If we don't or can't use it, then we worry about why we have it at all! Junk will get you—don't sit there and argue with yourself that it won't.

The most valuable "someday useful" junk will stymie your emotional freedom if not handled properly. Inasmuch as all of us feel guilty and frustrated about our pile of junk, we have to eliminate the problem. In turn, it will eliminate an unbelievable amount of "housework hours."

The Origin of Junk

There is a reason that we quit using something: It is outdated, broken, unsafe, unattractive, or inoperable. This simply means that we don't need it any more except, of course, for sentimental value. As each day goes by, it becomes more outdated, more unsafe, more unattractive, and will remain broken and inoperable. So learn to follow the 70-30 law that a magazine publisher made famous. He held up an ordinary magazine and said, "Look, 70% of this magazine is advertising." So anyone who has any magazines or papers lying in boxes or piles around the house has 70% junk. The first time you read a magazine, remove any article of interest to you and throw the 70% junk away. If you start doing this regularly, you'll rejoice for having eliminated those hernia-causing boxes of magazines (and besides, all those sculptured olives and individual hand-carved carrots we see in the pictures were meant to be bronzed, not eaten!). Instead of piles of magazines, you will have a thin, usable file of articles you want or need. Other junk can be treated the same way, and you'll see a great transformation.

The faucet leaks and the handles are corroded, so we replace them with a sleek new chrome beauty. Looking at the old ones longingly, we can't bear to throw them away because someday (even though they're broken, outdated, unsafe, unattractive, and inoperable) . . . we just might need a washer out of them. So we put them in the junk drawer or closet or shelf or hang them in the garage to get tangled up in the bicycle spokes. We could have removed the washers in two minutes and thrown the rest in the garbage, saving dozens of maintenance hours working around the old faucet. What a mighty grip junk has on us. We'll keep that worthless worn-out faucet for 15 years, then in our move to Denver or Boston or Phoenix, into a new house, guess what we take with us . . . yes, the old faucet. We never know when we might need it.

No matter how we may rationalize, "Oh well, there's nothing in the attic" or "We have plenty of room in the basement," that junk should go to the dump. The number one secret of proper junk disposal or dispersal is to make the decision *at the time something is to be put away or stored.* Because once you

store it, sentimental attachment and mental obligation to use it (to justify the storage) begin to mount. Another ruling factor in living efficiently with junk is facing reality as to just how much room is really available for storage. If you can't conveniently store an item, then logically you cannot use it conveniently. Often the storage cost is far higher than the replacement cost of an article.

The Economics of Storage

On a special contract assignment at a Sun Valley resort one year, my company furnished decorated Christmas trees to the guests. The year before, the previous installers lost $5,000 providing the decorated trees because they hired carpenters and highly paid laborers to adorn and take down the trees. We contracted it the next year. We bought the Christmas decorations and the trees wholesale. When the holiday season was over, the maid would call our office and a crew would pick up the trees, take off the light bulbs and metal stands, and pack and store them for the next year's use. When it all was totaled up, we lost only $900 the first year. Then we did some "storage strategy" thinking, and the following year we made over $2,000 clear profit with half the headaches. What was our secret? We just followed the basic rule of storage economy. When the Christmas holiday was over, instead of picking the trees up, undecorating them, sorting and packing the decorations, hauling them to the warehouse, etc., we just pitched the entire tree—light bulbs, tinsel, stand and all—into the garbage. The labor and storage costs saved more than we paid for the decorations!

Think about the storage problem in your home. A lot of that stuff you are storing is useless. It is a constant source of worry. Most of it is unsafe, outdated, and ugly, so why keep it? Why spend a valuable part of yourself polishing, washing, dusting, and thinking about it? YOU CAN'T AFFORD JUNK. It will rob

POSSESSION PROGRESSION

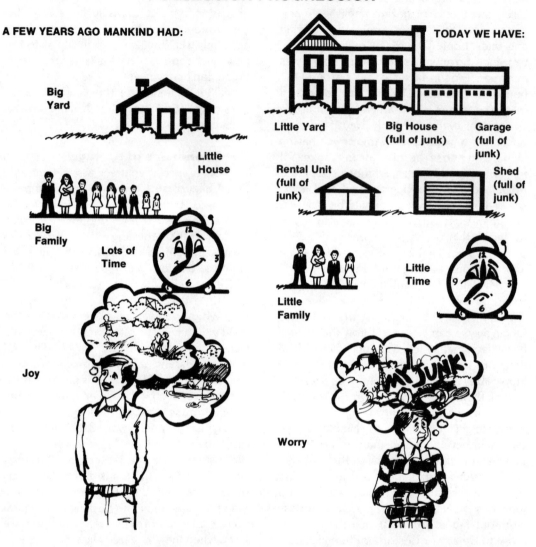

A FEW YEARS AGO MANKIND HAD:

Big Yard

Little House

Big Family

Lots of Time

Joy

TODAY WE HAVE:

Little Yard

Big House (full of junk)

Garage (full of junk)

Rental Unit (full of junk)

Shed (full of junk)

Little Family

Little Time

Worry

MY JUNK!

you physically, emotionally, and spiritually. Freeing yourself from junk will automatically free you from housework (and it won't take any soap and water either). If you'll just "de-junk" your home, the time you have left over in the course of a year will be enough to complete and pay for three credit hours in that college class you've always wanted to take. When I say de-junk, I don't mean sort your four cubbyholes of worthless stuff into 10

bags of worthless stuff!—or I'll tell on you!

Now don't say, "Oh, I know my junk has got to go, and one of these days, I'm going to. . . ." There are more reasons than housecleaning to de-junk your house (and your life). This might surprise you, but it's a reality: Many people are buried so deep in junk that their mates are unable to navigate the clutter to get to them. Your spouse can't give you attention and affection until he or she can find you. I've cleaned (or tried to clean) hundreds of homes where lonely, frustrated men and women, buried in junk, can't understand why they and their families aren't closer. Junk is the barrier! Junk (and junk projects and activities) prevents you from being free, available for affection or opportunity. Too often the things we save and store—for sentiment's sake or because they might be valuable someday—end up as tombstones for us. Boxes of mummified prom corsages and piles of corroded hub caps will bury you but good. Get rid of your junk!

To start your de-junking program, begin with yourself! At an all-day seminar I convinced the entire audience that junk is a universal problem, not the "other guy's" problem. I gave every member of the audience two minutes to gather just the junk they were carrying with them (pockets—purses—briefcases), offering a prize for the most unique collection of junk (they initialed it for proper identification). My son passed around a large drawer and in minutes it overflowed. What did I get, you wonder? (We all love other people's junk, don't we!) It was hilarious. It was all *junk!* Used flashbulbs, a 1976 calendar, old speeding tickets, partly eaten chocolate-covered peanuts, a roll of toilet paper, two-year-old food coupons, rocks and pebbles, expired membership cards, half a sock, Christmas lists (after, not before!), broken compacts and empty lipstick containers, lids (censored), (even worse)—tons of it—and I suspect they held back plenty on me! The winning lady had a whole bulging hankyful . . . and she was the best-dressed woman there! *Junk is a reality.*

If having piles, rooms, or buildings full of junk (even labeled "antique") is worth all those hours to shuffle it and all that mental energy to keep track of it, then unfortunately you value junk more than your time and freedom. If having a closet full of gleaming silver is worth four hours of polishing time a month, you enjoy impressing people more than you value your time and your freedom. The storage strategy message is simple: Nothing exists in and of itself. Everything has a cost to acquire and to maintain. The majority of the cost you pay with your time and energy. Eliminate the junk and excess around your house. It's simple, and one of the easiest ways to free yourself from household imprisonment.

☑ CHECK! BEFORE YOU CLEAN IT!

Some things aren't worth doing! Some can't be cleaned. Others will look tacky even when they're clean and orderly. Taking care of these items first will not only make cleaning and maintenance easier, but will make you feel better (which is sure to make cleaning easier). Eliminate or remove anything that bugs you—that's inconvenient, no longer functional, or you just don't like. *REMEMBER—the first principle of efficient cleaning is to not have to clean in the first place*—Do these before you start:

☐ Have plenty of convenient, roomy litter receptacles. You'll do less cleaning up and picking up.

☐ Alter any physical surface or appearance that you don't like. Paint it, sand it, cover it, or give it away.

☐ Eliminate furniture you don't use or need. It has no value and magnifies your cleaning chores.

☐ Eliminate excess playthings (children and adults). Unused tennis rackets, snowmobiles, motorbikes, TV games that have fallen from favor, old hobby supplies, puzzles with "only one piece missing."

☐ Repair every leaky faucet.

☐ Make every door, drawer and window slide or close easily.

☐ Adjust every shelf to suit what you want and need.

☐ Be sure you have enough towel racks.

☐ Label all panel/fuse boxes.

☐ Get rid of all shin and head bumpers (countertops, doors, and drawers that bash you every time you pass by, or straighten up).

☐ Be sure all closets have an adequate supply of hangers.

☐ Get anything that can be mounted off the floor.

☐ Repair/replace all damaged surfaces.

☐ Make sure your vacuum works perfectly.

☐ Make cleaning tools attractive. All other things being equal, choose tools that are attractive, in materials that appeal to you. Even if you can't afford redwood and stainless steel, you can keep your cleaning tools sharp and nice by painting and decorating and personalizing them—use your imagination.

5

What to Expect out of Your Husband and Your Children

On this one, I will gladly assume the role of the learner. When you find something that works the miracle of getting husbands and children to assume their rightful obligation in housework, I have left room for you to enter it in the book.

This lack of cooperation is a reality, all right . . . but it doesn't have to be. While doing a consulting study for a large Eastern school district, I was introduced to a quiet grade school cafeteria. At the stroke of noon, 420 children converged enthusiastically on the polished lunch room with trays and brown bags. Forty minutes later the room was quiet again, but not polished. It looked like a tornado had feasted instead of humans. Forks, food, and wrappers decorated the floor, the tables, chairs, walls, and even the light fixtures. When we were finishing the building tour *two hours later,* I noticed the janitor just finishing the cleaning. *Two full 30-gallon garbage cans* were required to contain the mess the janitor picked up from that lunchroom. The next day we were touring a similar school in town. It was a grade school with the same floor plan, same area, and 412 students. This time we arrived about 15 minutes after lunch ended—and the place was immaculate! The janitor was scooping up what appeared to be the final dustpan of debris. I was told by the guide that not only was it the last dustpan, *it was the only dustpan!* This janitor had spent 15 minutes restoring the room and filled only a small pan of dirt, while the janitor at the other school labored two hours in the same area, after the same number of children, and accumulated two garbage cans full. What was the difference? Same number of kids, same community, same size building—but . . . *not the same boss!*

It's not circumstance that causes you to have a garbage can house and spend two hours cleaning when you could spend 15 minutes. It's you! The only difference between the schools was the principals. The first principal allowed his students freedom to eat and leave a mess; the other principal allowed his students the freedom of eating and simply added the responsibility of cleaning up their own mess. "Anything you mess up, you clean up" was the fair and simple rule. That meant crumbs, drops, and dribbles on tables, chairs, and floors. It took each kid 15 seconds to perform the task and unquestionably taught and reinforced the most important ingredient of greatness: *responsibility.* Any woman who cleans up after a husband or a kid over two years old deserves the garbage cans she has to lug out every day!

I don't ordinarily suggest open rebellion or brute force, but I do offer these two suggestions:

1. Refuse to be the janitor for the kids' and husband's messes. Picking up after them is bad for everyone involved. You teach irresponsibility perfectly by assuming responsibility for someone else, except those who don't know any better or can't help themselves. Insist that everyone clean up his or her own messes and premises. Don't send husband to work or children to school undisciplined.

2. Write down and post needs. When you demand or ask for help, many family members will begin to assist you. Written messages eliminate short memories and the innocent phrase "I didn't know you needed anything done."

Sorry I can't help you more on this one!
P.S. My apologies to the 5% of husbands and children who do their share around the house.

6
Relax and Work Less

A big event was coming to a local small town and in preparation, the townspeople resolved to clean the hardwood floor in the village recreation center. It was decided to scrub all the dirt, finish marks, and old wax buildup from the floor and apply a coat of clear resinous finish (varnish). The committee in charge chose four of the best housecleaners and some husbands and the building janitor to do the job. It took the group of seven most of a Saturday to finish it. Six hours they labored, spending a total of 42 hours to get the floor ready for the finish application.

Four years later, after some hard use, the floor again needed the same attention. I had a free day, and since I consider cleaning floors an enjoyable pastime, I volunteered to do the job at no charge. I refused the help of other volunteering townspeople and the jani-

tor and instead used my sons, who were 12 and 8 years old. We showed up at the building at 10:30 and went home early for lunch at 11:45. The job was completed perfectly in 1¼ hours, or for the three of us 3¾ total hours, much less than the 42 hours used by the group. We used three fewer mops, half the cleaners and strippers, and a tenth of the hot water—and did a much better job.

Any of you could have done the same thing, using a valuable principle of cleaning: Relax and work less. To relate this principle more directly to the domestic front, let's take a glimpse of Betty Betterhouse in action.

It has been an unbelievable morning. In addition to her own seven children, 14 others, caught in a snowstorm, were overnight guests at her home. They consumed dozens of whole-wheat pancakes, eggs, and other breakfast goodies. It was two hours before Betty finally saw her guests depart and the children off to school. She then turned to the task of restoring her kitchen to livable condition. The drops of batter, jam and grease covering her stove and countertop were now dry, hard, and firmly stuck. Betty began scrubbing one end of the counter furiously. Finally loosening (or wearing away) the spattered batter in one spot, she would move on another few inches to grind some more of the droplets away. Fifteen minutes later, after exhausting effort, she had the counter presentable.

Eliminate—Saturate—Absorb!

She could have saved 13 minutes and at the same time preserved the countertop surface if she had used the cleaning principle that my sons and I used on the floor. You could call it the universal law of cleaning: *eliminate—saturate—absorb*. You can do 75% of your cleaning with your head, not your hands—because 75% of soil removal is done chemically, not by elbow grease. *Scrubbing* to clean something went out with beating your clothes on a rock by the riverside. Betty needs only to shovel or sweep the crust and loose food particles from the countertop *(eliminate:* 15 seconds). She should generously soak her dishcloth in soapy water and wet the entire area *(saturate:* 15 seconds), then give the liquid a few minutes to soak and loosen the spatters

(absorb). Then she merely has to wipe the mushy residue off. Two minutes for the total job. Of course, many of us have been doing this for years, not only on our countertops, but on floors, rugs, walls, light fixtures, automobiles, sinks, tubs, hardware, fireplaces, and 400 other places that might have used Betty's old time-consuming system. Hard soap crust on the bathroom sink where the hand soap sticks can take several minutes of scrubbing, but if it were sprayed or dampened first, it could be wiped off in two seconds. Almost everything will clean *itself* with water and the right chemical. Water is practically free and with a few cents' worth of chemicals it can replace numerous hours of your time if used with the principle outlined above. It is so easy to apply the right solution and wait. Leave. Read. Rest! Apply more solution in another area, or do anything you want while the solution dissolves and the chemical action loosens and suspends the dirt. Unless you get your kicks out of scrubbing, there is not much reason to scrub and grind soil off. By using the simple principle of *eliminate—saturate—absorb* in all cleaning, you can cut time and energy use as much as we cut the floor job for the town recreation center.

On your house floors, for example, remove the obvious large objects (such as forks, overshoes, yoyos, dog bones, etc.), then spread the solution in as large an area as you can handle before it dries out. As you are

The Basic Principle of Cleaning

When cleaning a floor, wall, stovetop, tub, or patio, apply the cleaning solution over as much of the area as possible.

Don't concentrate on tiny areas and scrub in one place.

Spread solution over a large area and let it soak in. By the time you get here, surface will have cleaned itself 70%.

finishing at one end of the room, the solution you first laid down is already working actively on the dirt, old wax, spots, stains, marks. When you return to the first area and begin to mop, wipe it clean, or lightly scrub, the remaining area is under heavy attack by the liquid, and most of the cleaning will have been accomplished by the time you get there with the mop.

When we cleaned the big floor in 1¼ hours we spent almost no time scrubbing. Solution was spread in working areas and I ran over the surface with a machine (or with a Doodle-bug). I didn't try to grind or scrub the floor clean, I covered it quickly to loosen the surface so the chemical solution could do the work. By the time I reached the far end of the room, the solution spread on the first part had dissolved and suspended the dirty old wax. The next trip over the same area caused every drop of dirt and wax to come off. The floor

generally your own fault—you've failed to perform good regular cleaning. Buildups of various kinds are the greatest obstacle to simple cleaning. This is best exemplified by the old villain hard water. Look at the brand-new sparkling tile in your shower, or your exterior windows. They are going to get water on them from use, accident, rain, or irrigation. The residue is an innocent thing called a *drop*. A drop doesn't seem much of a bother, because if unmolested, it will evaporate away.

At least it will appear to leave. A closer examination reveals that each drop has a character called mineral salts which slide to the bottom of the drop as it evaporates. Though the drop appears to have vanished, a slight deposit of mineral salts remains at the bottom. Beginning so insignificantly and unseen, it is ignored. Again water is splashed on the surface and new drops form in the place occupied by previous drops, and leave their

was immediately squeegeed and the gunk was picked up with a plain old dustpan and put in a bucket. This eliminated the need for a "slop mop." The floor squeegeed clean, then only needed to be mopped with clear water. One mop bucket did the whole floor!

In cases where all the dirt won't quite come off and scrubbing seems called for, it's

mineral marks to unite with the existing residue. Six months, 60 showers, or 20 lawn sprinklings later, that innocent first drop has become hard-water buildup. If kept clean daily, or in many cases, even weekly, it is a 2-minute instead of a 20-minute job. If done annually or "when I get around to it," it is a surface-damaging, chemical-squandering experience, greatly embittering one's attitude toward sanitation.

Be Sure to Touch Base

Be sure to match your cleaning agent base to the dirt or soil you are trying to remove. This is a simple but important principle. "Base" simply means dissolving agent. Water won't cut oil because it's the wrong base. Vinegar won't cut grease even for Merlin the Magician. Most household cleaners won't cut oil at all. An inexpensive oil-base solvent or thinner will dissolve it in seconds. When oil or tar get on walls, floors, rugs, or even clothes, a solvent (like paint thinner, turpentine, or other petroleum base cleaner) will break down the tar or oil so that they can be easily wiped away. You can rub and grind "contact cement edge slops" with every cleaner and mineral spirit available and not get anywhere. If you use a little lacquer thinner or contact cement solvent (again, *matching* the contact cement base), it is instantly softened and can be wiped off as easily as soft butter out of a dish! Cleaning preparation labels will generally give the base. Whenever you are in doubt as to whether a particular solvent should be used

on a particular surface, test it first in an inconspicuous area.

Abrasion Evasion

Using powdered cleansers and steel wool to grind dirt off surfaces has become a ritual with too many homemakers. With the same generosity they use to apply powder to the baby's rump, they coat their sinks with cleansing powder and attack them with brisk rubbing. You can actually hear the results as the grinding abrasion quickly removes stains and spots, along with the chrome or porcelain on the unit. The cleanser then has to be flushed off. Some of it will set like concrete in the gooseneck of the sink drain, on the floor, and on the fixtures. The light scum which remains on the sink or tub has to be rubbed and polished off, again wearing away the surface. The damage is gradual but inevitable. Even more important, you lose time cleaning by the abrasion method. You should be relaxing to the cleaning principle *eliminate—saturate-absorb*. It really works. Discipline yourself to use it, and you'll reward yourself with two hours of free time out of the four hours you once wasted grinding and scrubbing away!

7

Don't Be Caught Streaking . . . Windows

The dreaded task: At my housecleaning seminars I always spring the question, "How many of you like to clean windows?" This is always good for a chorus of groans from everyone present. Occasionally, about two out of every thousand will raise an eager hand indicating that they, indeed, enjoy cleaning windows. (Further investigation reveals why: Both have maids to do the job!) That leaves almost 100% of homemakers who hate window cleaning.

The reason is quite simple. After hours of laboriously polishing windows, you think "At last. I'm finished!" Hope is dashed when the sun comes up or changes angle. Streaks, sheens, and smears suddenly appear out of nowhere, magnified for all to see. In instant anger, you again give the window the old college try, and the smears, streaks, and sheens only change places. Rearming yourself with more window cleaner, rags, and gritty determination, you work even harder and faster to get the windows clean, but they seem only to get worse. Night falls, and so does the curtain,

Spraying and rubbing is self-defeating—as you can see as soon as the sun comes up or changes direction.

rescuing a crestfallen and discouraged worker. The next morning you go downtown and eye the 50-story, solid-glass-window buildings, the huge storefront display windows, and mumble, "That glass is beautiful . . . but I never see anyone cleaning it. How do they ever do it so fast and so well?"

The reason we seldom see window cleaners is not because those windows don't need to be done. Most commercial windows have to be cleaned more often than house windows. But professional window cleaners only take minutes, not hours, to do their job. Homemakers can be just as effective on their own windows if they learn and practice some of the basic techniques used by the professionals.

The first move toward successful window cleaning is to rid your storage cabinet of all the "glass gleam" garbage you have been trying to make work for years. The paramount reason your windows streak and seem to get worse is the oily, soapy gunk you've been spraying on them. Pounds of it have been sprayed on, and only part of it wipes off. Gradually you have built a base of transparent waxy material which you move and spread around every time you try to clean the window. It not only creates an impossible cleaning situation, it also primes the glass surface to absorb and hold dust, bug spots, and airborne particles. The result is windows that have to be cleaned more often.

Take heart. It hasn't been your fault all these years. Even the chief window washer for New York City's tallest all-glass buildings couldn't get windows clean without streaks if all he used was the gunk sold to most of the public.

To recover all those lost polishing hours, let's learn to do windows professionally. Go down to the janitorial supply house and buy a professional brass or stainless steel squeegee with a 10-, 12-, or 14-inch blade. Ettore Steccone brand is the best! Don't go to the local supermarket or discount house and buy those reconditioned-truck-tire war clubs they call "squeegees." They will not work well, even in a professional's hands.

Pick up some window-cleaning solution, which can be ordinary liquid dish detergent, ammonia, or trisodium phosphate. All will work well if you use them sparingly. There is always a tendency to add too much chemical or soap solution, which causes streaks and leaves residue. One lid or capful is plenty for each gallon of warm water.

Get a professional squeegee. Make sure it laps over ends.

Keep rubber blade undamaged. Don't beat kids or squeegee floor with it.

Long handles are available.

Four Steps to Sparkling Windows

1. Using a clean sponge, soft-bristle brush, or a wand applicator, lightly wet the window with the cleansing solution. You don't need to flood it away. You're cleaning it, not baptizing it! If the window is really dirty or has several years of miracle gunk built up, go over the moistened area again.

2. Quickly wipe the dry rubber blade of your newly purchased squeegee with a damp cloth or chamois. The reason for using a damp cloth is that a dry blade on any dry glass area will "peep-a-peep" along and skip places. Dampening the blade lubricates it.

3. Next, tilt the squeegee at an angle, pressing one end of the squeegee lightly against the top of the window *glass* (not the house shingles or the window frame) and pull the squeegee across the window horizontally (see illustration). This will leave about a 1-inch dry area across the top of the window. Remember all those drips that came running down from the top of your clean window when you tried squeegeeing once before? Well, by squeegeeing across the top, you've removed that potential stream.

4. Wipe the squeegee blade again with the damp cloth and place the rubber blade horizontally in the dry area and then pull down, lapping over enough into the dry, clean area to avoid any surplus water running in the cleaned area. Wipe the squeegee after each pass.

A window can be cleaned from either side or from the top using this technique. Always be sure to angle off the top edge of the glass to eliminate potential dripping. Wipe off the bottom of the window sill with your damp cloth.

It's worth the effort to work on this for awhile, since it will be awkward at first. All of that accumulated gunk might take a little extra effort to remove. Once you catch on, you'll love it and wish you had more windows to do.

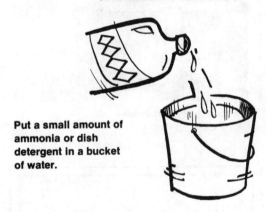

Put a small amount of ammonia or dish detergent in a bucket of water.

Step 1.

Wet window lightly with brush or sponge.

Step 2.

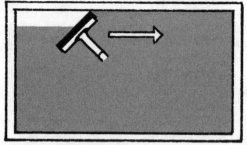

Then angle-cut the top edge of the window with the squeegee. This will stop top drip.

Step 3.

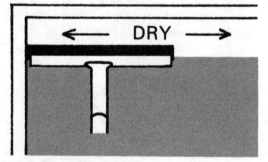

Place squeegee in dry area—

Step 4.

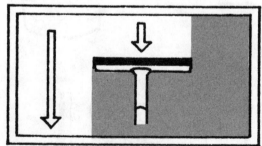

and pull down to clean. Wipe squeegee with damp cloth or chamois after each pass.

How to get rid of those last spots. After completing a window, you undoubtedly will detect a tiny drop or squeegee mark or two and a little moisture on the 1/8-inch area where the side of the glass meets the frame. Your old tendency was to snatch a dry cloth and with a fingertip under it wipe off the edge. I can assure you this will leave a 3/4-finger-wide mark right down that edge. Once you notice that, the temptation will be to wipe it again, this time with a bundled cloth. Then you'll have a four-inch mark and have to clean the whole window again. After squeegeeing the window, just leave those 1/8-inch beads of side moisture. They will disappear and you'll never see them. Your friends won't, either, unless they bring their opera glasses with them. As for middle-of-the-window drops or tiny squeegee lines, do not use a cloth (**Law:** There is no such thing as a lint-free or mark-free cloth in window cleaning). Because you've been working in the solution, your bare hand will be oil-free and by the time you get a window finished will be dry enough to dry wipe marks away without leaving a blemish.

This method is as easy as it sounds. It's three to five times faster than the old way. It will use only a penny or two worth of cleaner and leave your windows pure and clean to repel particles and dirt. Remember, atmospheric conditions affect glass more than any other material in the house: thus windows are a prime surface for film, oil, dirt, and even fingerprints. Try to keep your windows so clean and slick that flies lose their footing. Slick, squeaky glass will repel marks much better than glass with a coat of wax or soap scum on it.

Problem Areas

Squeegees will work on any normal household window (not on textured or stained glass, for instance), and they come in sizes to fit the task at hand. Squeegees can be cut to custom-fit your windows if you so desire. For small Victorian-style panes, a squeegee can be cut down with a hacksaw to fit. Pull the rubber out of the channel before cutting, and always cut the rubber a wee bit longer than the remodeled blade.

Avoid the temptation to use a cloth to wipe the last few drops of water off a squeegeed window. Your bare, oil-free hand will do much better.

My advice regarding those tiny little square windows is to let them go as long as possible, because optical illusion from the concentrated small squares hides marks, specks, and smudges. When they do need cleaning, depending on their size either a squeegee or a trigger spray bottle with diluted evaporating (alcohol base) window cleaner can be used. If you're not too particular, I'd just hose them down, brush off the outside, rinse them, and call it good. I don't think any window in a home is worth numerous hours of work. Big windows show dirt and streaks more readily than small panes. Small panes look more "romantic" a bit hazy.

There are times and places in small, confined areas where a spray bottle with an alcohol-base, evaporating-type solution is more efficient to use (handprints on glass entrance doors, mirrors, decorative doors and windows, etc.). An inexpensive window-cleaning solution obtained in concentrated form from a janitorial supply house is diluted with water and sprayed lightly on soiled glass, then buffed dry with a cotton cloth. The quick-drying solution won't leave a waxy buildup and it allows you to "polish" the glass. Only slight sheens and streaks are left, which are seldom noticeable in such small areas.

When window casings and trim get older, paint and mortar chips catch under the squeegee blade and make cleaning miserable. New aluminum or well-maintained wood won't give you any grief. If your squeegee blade gets damaged and leaves a line, turn it over. When it wears out or rounds out, just buy a new rubber and snap it into the squeegee channel. (Be sure 1/8 inch of the rubber blade laps over at each end of the channel.)

When windows are out of reach for easy hand or ladder work, a pole or handle of any length you can maneuver will work on the same principle with surprising accuracy. I use a 4- to 8-foot Ettore Steccone extending handle. Clean glass always looks good. A few tiny smudges or drips won't hurt anything, so don't try to be a perfectionist. It isn't worth the stress or time.

The Bionic Man & Wonder Woman are the only ones who can go through glass unharmed!

The rest of us have to be careful.

Other Window Problems

Don't let hard water get on your windows. If it has, don't use abrasive cleanser or the glass will cloud and scratch. There are some mild phosphoric acid cleaners on the market that will remove the deposit. Once you've done that, keep hard water off with regular maintenance or an adjustment in your sprinkling system.

45

Most window damage (aside from breaking them) occurs when labels are being removed from new windows or paint or mortar from new or old ones. There are three rules in performing cleanup operations on glass:

Buy a good sealed, double-glazed unit such as Thermapane.

. . . not a 3-section storm window with 6 sides to clean!

1. Always keep the glass surface wet. The foreign material you are trying to remove will then generally slide or float off instead of digging in.

2. Use only razor-sharp blades or flat razor-type tools in a one-way forward motion, then lift the tool off the glass and make another forward stroke. Never go back and forth. Pulling the tool back and forth will eventually trap a piece of grit or sand behind and under the blade, which will scratch even a wet window (you'll never rub *that* one off with a de-oiled bare hand, either).

Dragging scraper back can trap sand or dirt under blade causing it to scratch the glass.

3. Don't use abrasive scrub pads or compounds on window glass.

Learning to clean windows fast and effectively will change your outlook on life. You'll cherish the cute little handprints, enjoy watching frustrated insects slip off the glass, and even tolerate the sweet birdies who occasionally befoul your windows.

Prevention—Keeping the Enemy Out

8

What do we do with the dirt on the
    farm?
It flies from the road and comes
    straight from the barn.
It pours through the windows.
It tracks on the floors.
We just give up and plant our garden
    indoors.

—Marilyn May

Mats: A Must

A new modern hospital, nestled in a valley with one of the world's most famous ski
resorts, had been in operation for two years
when its housekeeping personnel retired. Re-
placements were needed and a professional
cleaning service was contracted. Following
careful measurement of the space, occu-
pancy, conditions, and with direction from the
retiring staff members, it was concluded that a
total of 12 hours of work was required each
night to clean the whole: offices, public area,
entrances, and medical administrative wing.
When signing the contract, the owner of the
janitorial company made one explicit demand. Both entrances to the hospital were to
be covered with a nylon, vinyl-backed mat,
covering at least 15 feet inside both entrances. There had been no mats before because aesthetically they were a possible dis-
traction from the hospital's alpine beauty. The
hospital's administrator agreed to order the
doormats that day.

The cleaning company began their service and were spending 12 hours plus a few extra daily to keep the place up to standards. They wet-mopped nightly, used six treated dustcloths on the floor, and had to scrub some areas every week with their machines. Anticipating the difference the new mats would make, the cleaning company owner had the sweeping and vacuuming crew keep and photograph the night's residue collected from the floor throughout the building. Each night a gallon can was half-filled with gravel, sand, thread, pine needles, and every other possible thing common to a resort area. Three weeks later, the mats arrived and were installed at both entrances.

The first night the mats were in place, the hours of work dropped to 10, and the sweeping residue was reduced to half a quart of gum wrappers, toothpicks, etc. After one week, the new mats reduced the cleaning to 9 hours per night. The dustcloths were reduced from six to two, mopping was reduced to two times a week, and dusting to every other night. Cleaning supplies were cut more than 50%. The mats cost $240 and they were paid for in less than one week in labor and cleaning supplies saved. No increase in entrance falls was noted, and the mats lasted for four years!

Proper matting alone could save the average household 200 hours of work a year, slow down structure depreciation 7%, and save $160 in direct cleaning supply costs. The cost of matting for the average home is approximately $80. But it's the 200 hours that's the big savings for you. That's 30 minutes a day cut from your chore time with no effort expended.

The reasons for such savings of time, effort, money, and depreciation are easy to understand if you simply ask yourself, "What is it that I clean out of my house, off my rugs, off the walls, off the pictures, upholstery, etc." Dust and dirt are the obvious answers. Where does it come from? Almost 100% of it comes from the outside. How does it get inside?

Eighty-five percent of it *is transported in* (the rest leaks through cracks, is airborne, or originates inside). Most dirt or residue is carried into the home via the clothes and the feet. Where is your carpet the dirtiest? At the entrance, on about a 3x4-foot square where the matting should be. It's only logical—if dirt doesn't get in, you won't have to round it up. As a person criticizing mats once said, "Bah! I hate doormats—all they are is dirt catchers!" I rest my case.

Taking advantage of good matting is the smartest, easiest, and least expensive thing you can do to cut your housecleaning time. It is easier to vacuum or shake out a mat daily than it is to chase dirt all over the house. Look at the hospital. The distributed dirt and debris were reduced from one half-gallon to one pint. Mats will perform a great service in your home. Convinced? Don't take my word for it—try it! You'll cry over the lost years of labor and money you've wasted by not getting adequate mats sooner. Instead of scrubbing your floor weekly, you could end up doing it annually. (I've even had one commercial building

PROPER MATTING WILL:

1. **Keep your house cleaner.**
2. **Reduce frequency of carpet shampooing, floor washing and waxing.**
3. **Provide sound absorption.**
4. **Enhance safety.**
5. **Improve appearance.**

go *five years* and the floor finish still looked good.) If you have good matting, all the fine gravel, grit, and dirt that hangs on the bottom of the shoe and scratches, soils, and discolors will be out of action. Waxed floors last a long time when they aren't abused by grit. Next time you go into an office building, notice the difference in the floor on the lower level as compared to the upper-level floors, even though the traffic might be the same. The upper ones will last twice as long and look twice as good because the grit doesn't get to them. Traffic doesn't hurt a floor much—it's the abrasiveness of dirt that creates havoc. Keep it out of your home, and you'll keep yourself out of the crouching, scrubbing position.

Here are some matting pointers that will advance your goal of gaining 30 "free" minutes a day:

Some mats to sidestep. Avoid decoration mats. We all love to see our name in print—even on a tiny, worthless rubber doormat. Get rid of it! It isn't doing much good, and the time it takes to clean around it is probably greater than the cleaning time it saves. Link mats (the kind made from little slices of old car tires laid on their sides and spliced with wire) are ineffective for most homes and extremely dangerous for wearers of high heels. Cocoa mats are more trouble than they're worth because they don't absorb well. Have you ever tried to clean a cocoa mat? That alone should convince you not to buy one!

For outside the house, the synthetic-grass-type mats or any rough, nonperforated mat with a rubber back is good. These won't rot, they're easy to clean, and they'll knock the big stuff off the shoes or boots of the person coming into your home. Try to get a 4x5-foot or longer mat to cover three or four steps. The exact type of exterior mat to buy depends on the space available, overhead cover (awning or porch), if any, your home and landscaping style, and how bad thievery is in the neighborhood.

On the inside: The first thing to do is get rid of any carpet samples or scraps you are using for "throw rugs." These items are, indeed, appropriately named. The jute backing and curling edges throw their users into the hospital. They're unsafe, unattractive, and more important, inefficient. Get rid of them!

At any janitorial supply house, you can buy commercial-grade, vinyl/rubber backed

Avoid using cheap carpet squares.

Don't use clothbacks.

Get rid of link or perforated mats.

49

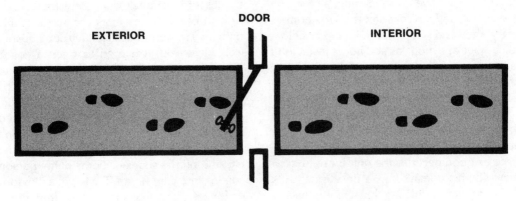

Try to allow 4 steps on each mat

EXTERIOR   DOOR   INTERIOR

Use commercial, nylon-tuft mats inside. These mats are
available in a wide range of colors and can be obtained in rolls
or in pre-cut sizes at a commercial janitorial supply house.

nylon mats. They are efficient, will last for years, and are available in a wide variety of colors. They come in widths of three, four, or six feet, and in any length. The nylon creates a static charge that actually helps pull particles from your shoes and clothes. They will absorb mud and water from foot traffic and hold it in the roots of the mat. They won't show dirt easily and can be vacuumed like any other carpet. When they need washing down, take them out to the sidewalk; spray with a hose; sprinkle a little cleaning solution on them and brush it around. Then rinse them and hang them out to dry.

Some mats will creep a little, and a "rug

**Design doors
for clearance.**

hugger" type can be purchased if you get tired of retrieving the carpet. This type of mat for inside areas of the home helps to reduce falls and trap loose dirt. The trapped dirt is the same dirt you would have to be cleaning from everything in the house.

An often forgotten area in our homes which should also be well matted is the garage entrance. Husbands and children transport plenty of sawdust, oil stains, and project residue into the house from the garage. Fine silt, sand, and gravel piled up on the road often get caught up in the snow which lodges under a car and falls loose on the garage floor. When it melts, the sand and grit are carried into the house by foot. Concrete dust and garage-type soils and dirt are abrasive to carpet or waxed floors.

Apartments, condominiums, and motor homes are not excluded from the need for mats. The slightly smaller amount of dirt/ debris that might get to the eighth floor of a modern apartment is multiplied by the fact that it has a smaller area over which to distribute itself, hence the soiling and damage to the dwelling can be as acute as in a large, dust-surrounded farmhouse.

To maintain mats . . .

1. Hose and scrub away dirt.

2. Squeegee off excess water and hang to dry.

Hang to dry—never use when back is wet.

3. Keep vacuumed.

A 3x5-foot mat is an excellent all-purpose size. It's wide enough to cover an average doorway, long enough to cover four entrance steps, and light enough to handle and to clean. An extra 3x12-foot "runner" may be rolled up and kept for remodeling, parties or wet weather. This extra mat would be a good investment if your traffic, lifestyle, and location merit it. It would be especially good for a new home. It's common for a family to move in before the landscaping is com-

pleted. The several months of working on the yard generates a lot of mud, and the resulting damage is often unnoticed because the house is new.

Along with the 30 minutes a day you will save when you install adequate matting, you gain aesthetic value, safety benefits, sound absorption, and even an inviting place for Rover and Tabby to bed down. Get mats before you start to clean, and you won't have to start as soon or work as long.

9

Floors Under Your Foot and Rule

The floor, more than any other part of the house, projects the overall image of your home. The chances of anyone's noticing that all-day sucker stuck to the patio door, the half-eaten wiener on the bookcase, or the cobweb across Grandpa's picture, are lessened if the floors are clean and brilliant. And maintaining beautiful floors is one of the simplest jobs in the house.

The term "hard floors" did not originate as a description of the effort needed to clean them; it's simply used to distinguish them from soft floors and carpets. Hard floors include tile, linoleum, wood, ceramic tile, terrazzo, cork, dirt (nothing under it), and good old concrete. All hard floors have their purpose and place, and they all have to be cleaned and maintained.

Good floor care can be a lifesaver for you physically and emotionally. There are four reasons for you to learn and apply proper floor care practices:

1. **Appearance.** A beautiful floor is an exhilarating experience for the beholder and a reward for the homemaker.

2. **Protection.** Even the hardest surfaces will scuff, wear, and dull with grinding foot traffic, spills and chemical cleaners. A wax or other protective finish covering the surface lessens the abrasions and other damage and lengthens the life of a floor. Even the new "no-wax" floors *do* need a dressing or finish to prevent an eventually dull surface.

3. **Cleanability.** Soil, dirt, spills, marks of all kinds, and abrasive residues are much sim-

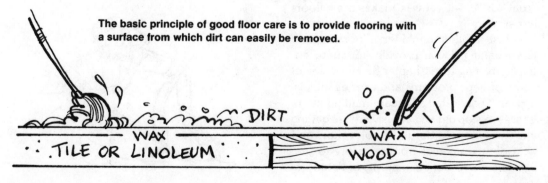

The basic principle of good floor care is to provide flooring with a surface from which dirt can easily be removed.

pler to clean from a well-waxed or finished surface. Sweeping a well-used unwaxed or unfinished tile floor will take you 25% longer than sweeping a highly polished, smooth-surfaced one. A coat of wax on the floor is like a coat of varnish on a bare wood picnic table. It keeps the soils and greases from penetrating the surface. Wiping something from the top of a nonpenetrable finish takes only seconds. It sure beats spending hours trying to scrub it out when it has soaked in and stained.

4. **Safety.** Contrary to what most people think, shiny, well-waxed and properly maintained floors are generally much less slippery than bare floors. Bare, worn floors have a flint-hard surface when wet, dry, or slick. A coat or two of wax or finish actually cushions the floor. It could be compared to laying a thin cloth or cover over the top of a bare plastic

DANGEROUS   **SAFE**

Clean, waxed floors are safer than
bare, untreated floors because wax
creates a cushion.

table top: The cover creates a cushion or surface that won't let things slide around. Thus a "coat" or "cover" of wax makes most floors less slippery.

Just another reminder: Floors require less cleaning if you provide adequate entrance matting (see Chapter 8). Hundreds of hours of floor problems and worries will disappear if you install adequate matting at entrances to stop dirt and abrasives from getting into your house. Some discoloration and wear of waxes comes from exposure to sunlight and aging. But the majority of deteriora-

tion of floors and discoloration of wax or finish comes from penetration of dirt into the wax and the floor surface.

How to Clean Hard Floors

The tools and equipment needed to clean your floors depend on the amount and type of hard-surface floors you have. During the last 20 years, carpet has found its way into more and more of the new houses built, often leaving only kitchen and bathroom with hard floors. If a hard floor is in the center of the house where considerable travel over carpeted areas is required to reach it, that hard-floor finish will last for months (if kept clean), and you could do it by hand in about 15 minutes a year.

If you have several rooms of tile, vinyl, linoleum, quarry tile, and wood-surfaced floors as well as a big game room, garage, converted patio, or storage area, some basic laborsaving floor tools would be a good investment. The chart in Chapter 2 outlines what I would suggest. Get a good 16-ounce mop, preferably rayon layflat, and a good mop bucket with a built-in roller-type wringer (Geerpress #180 is a nice one). Wringing mops by hand is "finger suicide." The pins, glass, etc., your mop picks up will lacerate your hands. The price of a small commercial mop bucket might shock you, but gasp once or twice and buy it anyway. It will be a time-saver and greatly contribute to the quality of work you can do.

Keep It Clean

Again, the most important factor in saving time and keeping maintenance of your floor to a minimum is simple: Keep it clean! That doesn't just mean removing roller skates, doggie bones, coins, combs, and clothes, either. It is the dust, grit, gravel, sand, food crumbs, and other such substances which remain on floors and eventually get ground into powder and embed themselves in your floor that cause your cleaning woes. Once all this "dirt power" is on the loose, it will destroy a floor rapidly. Keep hard floors well swept (even when you can't see dirt and dust). Where possible, use a commercial 18-inch treated dustmop. It is faster, more effective, and will last much longer than anything you can pick up at the supermarket.

Thoroughly shake out your mop after every use, preferably not over your neighbor's fence.

Wax It!

As I said earlier, most hard floors need a protective coating. Floors will wear out much faster if they are not protected. Floors claiming to be "no-wax" will also dull in traffic areas if not protected by a finish of some kind. The "never need to wax" claim is false if you expect such a floor to stay shiny in heavy traffic areas.

First, Take the Old Wax Off

Once the hard floor is prepared by sweeping and you know the old wax or finish is due to come off, it's time to make that hard job an easy one. Arrive at the scene with a mop bucket three-quarters full of clean water. Don't put cleaner in the mop bucket. Depending on the size of the room, mix in an ordinary bucket some warm water and floor cleaner. Ammonia or detergent cleaner will do fine, or, if you want all the wax off, use a heavier ammonia solution or a commercial wax remover. Dip your fresh mop into the solution in the

Clean your floors following the same principle used on walls.

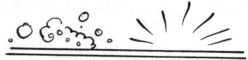

Be sure to rinse off soap and residue.

ordinary bucket (not the mop bucket) and apply to the floor generously so that the solution can attack the old wax or dirt. Cover as large an area as you feel you can clean and take up before it dries. You'll learn how much to do if it dries on you once. Remember, you are using the basic principle of cleaning explained in Chapter 6. As soon as the solution is on the floor old wax and dirt begin to be dissolved and suspended, and can soon be wiped off easily.

This is a bit optimistic, because chances are you have some spots where wax is built up thick as cardboard and hard as a bullet. It will need scrubbing and possibly another coat or two of solution. If so, scrub. If you don't have a floor machine, you can scrub away until the surface is free of everything you wish to remove. If you haven't got a machine, get a Doodlebug (3M makes the best). A Doodlebug has a handle (like a mop) with a plastic

Wax stripping:
Floor pads and nylon scouring pads are strong and effective.

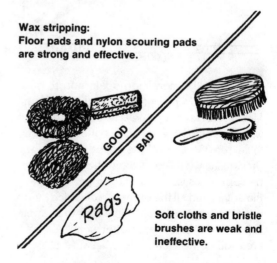

Soft cloths and bristle brushes are weak and ineffective.

"gripper" on its end which holds a flat 5x10-inch abrasive nylon floor pad. By applying a little weight to the handle, you can scrub the floor effectively. Edges, especially, are easy with a Doodlebug. I think one Doodlebug is superior to five of those small electric twin-brush scrubbers. If you use a floor machine, use nylon scrubbing pads under it. Brushes are almost worthless.

When the solution on the floor looks gunky and creamy, it means that dirt and old wax are coming loose. Check the scrubbed floor with your fingernail. If, after a scrape across the floor, you nail looks like your son's, then wax is still there. Scrub more and use more solution. As you are scrubbing and are on the verge of passing out from ammonia fumes and exhaustion, you are in a good frame of mind to resolve not to let your floor

Wax in traffic areas

Keep extra wax off edges. It won't wear off but will build up and yellow.

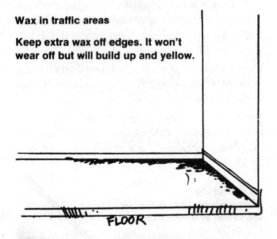

FLOOR

ever get in this condition again and to save yourself hundreds of future scrubbing hours. Most floor-cleaning time is spent trying to get wax off unused areas, such as under the lamp table, the TV, and off the edges of the floors. Previously, when you waxed the traffic paths or worn areas which needed it, you also gave the edges and all the other places which didn't need it a generous coat. This system of application is repeated year after year. A traffic area will come clean easily because there is

no buildup, but the thick areas will need lots of work to get the buildup off. Next time, don't wax the floors where you don't use them. Once you've given the entire area one coat of wax and more coats are to be applied, put the wax *on traffic areas only*.

Now, back to cleaning the floors. The floor is soaked and scrubbed, the wax and dirt

Be sure floors are dry before plugging in appliances!

are loosened, and it is a mess. Don't pull out that mop and try to sop or slop it up. Instead, reach for a simple, inexpensive tool called a floor squeegee. Get the 18-inch push-pull type (Ettore Steccone), not the heavy garage type, or use an old squeegee you have lying around (not your nice new window squeegee, which should be used only for windows). Squeegee the gunk into a puddle on the un-cleaned area, and use an ordinary dustpan and empty bucket to quickly scoop the gunk up. The clean, squeegeed area will be almost perfect. The squeegeed floor area (except for a possible drop or two from the squeegee lap) will be almost perfectly clean. A squeegee will give you one of the best possible jobs on floor coverings that have those little indentations—design impressions of various kinds. (Such floors are the "pits" to clean, for the most part. If you have a wet-dry vac, use it instead!) Now for the mop. Rinse it in clear water and then

56

damp-mop the area. Don't damp-mop where gunk puddles were. Let the floor dry, and that area is ready to wax. Repeat this process until the whole floor is finished. All the gunk will end up in one bucket to be dumped in the toilet (*not the sink*). The mop water will remain fresh and will work for the entire floor because it only rinses the squeegeed floor.

A hard commercial self-polishing finish (wax) won't mark easily. Soft wax requires more work.

When the floor is dry, apply a first light coat of wax on the entire floor. On the next coat and remaining ones, keep wax out of areas not used for traffic. I would use a good commercial interlock polymer finish, obtainable at any janitorial supply house.

Remember Daily Maintenance for Protection

After you've expended all the time and effort to get the floors clean and shiny, keep them clean daily and they will last for years. Remember, it's the spills, crumbs, sand, dust, etc., that create the conditions that make you work. If a few black marks get on the floor, they will be on top of the wax, and easily removed with the moist nylon cleaning pad on the end of your Doodlebug. Again, I will stress that the most efficient way to keep hard floors clean is on a daily basis with a good dustmop. Brooms stir up dust all over the place and leave fine unseen particles that will be ground into your new wax, eventually destroying the floor. A good dustmop is much faster and does a much better job than straw brooms.

A small, treated, commercial dust mop—18" or 24"—will pay you dividends.

It cleans hard-surfaced floors better and faster than any broom.

There is no comparison, especially if you have a good-quality mop. "Supermarket" dust-mops are a joke; they do more spreading than cleaning. Secure a good 18-inch commercial dustmop with a full-circle, rotating swivel head. This unit will cover a lot of ground quickly and is flat enough to get under furniture. It will gather gravel, paper clips, gum wrappers, safety pins, and the hundred other items that find their way to the floor, and will pick up and hold the dust. A dustmop is unbelievable on sealed concrete basement and garage floors. You'll have to buy a little dustmop (oil) treatment and spray the mophead when it is dry. Always spray 12 hours or more before use (even if you only have to spray it once a year) so that the oil has time to penetrate into all the fibers. If you have only a small amount of hard flooring, do it by hand with a cleaning cloth or dust cloth. You won't need a commercial dustmop.

Damp-mopping. Damp-mopping floors on a daily basis is fast and easy. Just fill the mop bucket half full of warm water and put in a little neutral cleaner. (I'd use a disinfectant cleaner.) If you get the cleaning solution too strong, it might "cut" or cloud the wax or finish. Dip the mop or a sponge mop, wring it slightly in your self-contained roller bucket, leave the mophead damp, and mop in a figure 8 pattern. Remember, the bathroom floor is small; it's not worth carrying a big mop and bucket into such close quarters. Do it in one minute with your spray bottle of disinfectant cleaner and wiping cloth.

Coping with Concrete Floors

Dustmopping concrete floors (mentioned above) is a trick most of us haven't heard of or used. Concrete floors, believe it or not, are almost equal in square footage to carpet in many American homes. Unfinished full basements are common. They wait many years—"until we can afford to finish those two bedrooms and a family room in the basement." Two-car garages are also a mass of concrete flooring. Both of these areas bear a constant flow of traffic back and forth into the "finished" part of the house. Concrete produces much destructive material (dirt, grit, etc.) and is responsible for more cleaning time than you might realize. The surface of concrete (which is made of sand, cement, lime, and additive) will perpetually "bleed" dust and grit, which if not cleaned up regularly, eventually circulates through your house.

Go get your broom right now and sweep your basement or garage. Leave the pile of residue, and go back and sweep again just as carefully. The second pile will amaze you, as will the third if you sweep it again. Because concrete is textured and porous and "bleeds," vacuuming it is really the only way to get it dustless, and after use, it will again be dusty. If you want to eliminate hundreds of hours of direct and indirect adverse results from concrete floors in your home, "seal" the concrete. You've walked on many a sealed floor in supermarkets, malls, stadiums, on ramps, etc. It looks like it is varnished. Sealed concrete is easy and practical to maintain and will last for years.

You can seal your own concrete floors. Concrete has to cure 28 days or longer after pouring before it's ready to seal. It's best to seal it before it's used, because oil stains and other fluids may penetrate and are not removable, and the seal will magnify any marks. On old or new concrete, sweep up all surface dirt and remove everything possible from the floor (furniture, tools, etc.). Mop on a solution of *strong, alkaline cleaner,* or better still, *etching acid* diluted in water. (Your janitorial supply house or paint store will have these.) Let it soak in a while. It will break and release the surface lime and debris on the concrete, leaving a good firm clean base. If the floor is old and marked, scrub it with a floor machine (or your trusty Doodlebug). Even if you can't scrub, apply the solution and let it set. Then flush the solution off, using your floor squeegee. Rinse with a hose. Allow the floor to dry for five or more hours. Transparent concrete seal or all-purpose seal can be obtained at paint stores or janitorial supply houses. (I have even used a gym-floor finish on two of my houses.) Apply it, according to directions, with any applicator that will distribute it in a nice thin even coat, and let it dry. Most concrete seals are self-leveling so it will turn out okay. I'd advise a second coat to make sure all the "etched," rough surfaces are filled. (Don't try to save the used applicator. Lamb's wool isn't worth cleaning out.)

Once the seal is dry, you have a shiny, glossy, smooth (not slick) surface which can be waxed or treated like any hard floor. Stains, oil slicks, etc., can be wiped off without leaving the usual ugly penetrating mark. Sealed concrete finish wears well. Chips and scrapes can be touched up with a small paintbrush or cloth and they will blend in. You can maintain sealed concrete floors just like other hard floors.

Wood Floors

Keep a good resinous finish or wax on your wood floor or follow dealer's recommendations. Moisture won't bother wood if a finish repels it. Once water or moisture gets into wood, it swells the grain and pops off the

Keep wood floors covered with protective varnish or other resinous floor finish.

BARE   FINISH

If moisture penetrates wood it swells, cracks, blisters, and wears.

outer finish. Then the wood deteriorates rapidly. Most wood floors can be treated like any hard-surface floor if the surface finish is adequate.

Avoid sanding wood floors. An eighth of an inch of wood taken off a ¾-inch floor really affects its performance. Cracks will appear and squeaks will develop.

If your wood floors are old- and ugly-looking, chances are the problem's not the wood, but the layers of yellowed, cracked finish. If you sand it down, the old finish will gum up the belts of the sander, and it will be a mess. Instead, try this easy way that works almost every time: Buy a gallon or two of varnish remover or paint remover, and apply generously to the floor. The old varnish will instantly crumble and release its hold on the wood. Use your trusty floor squeegee to mop up the mess and get rid of it. This should leave

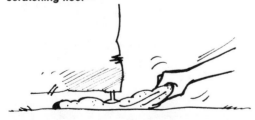

To move furniture easily without scratching floor—

A thick towel will slide and ease the unit for cleaning access.

the floor bare. Without leaving water on the floor for too long, clean it as previously instructed. This cleaning will get rid of any stripper residue left. If residue is not completely removed, future varnish applications will be adversely affected. Let the floor dry for 10 hours or until any swelling is gone. Touch up with a sanding disc or a little hand-sanding if there is a nick or two. Ignore small cracks and marks. The seal you apply will blend things in. Apply one coat of penetrating "seal" and one coat of finish. You won't believe how good it will look or how easy the job will be. Dealers of all these products have the directions on how to use them.

A Few Final Words About Floors

Remember, good matting at exterior and interior entrances will save you more floor work than all the gimmicks, tips, and miracle floor formulas combined. Avoid "one-stroke" miracle combinations that clean and wax your floor at the same time. If anyone in the family has shoes or other footwear that leave black marks, I would make a quick Salvation Army donation of them (the shoes, not the person!).

Some floors are much easier to maintain than others, so don't break your neck trying to match your neighbors'. Some floor material, because it is cheap, damaged, porous, or has bad color, is almost impossible to make look good.

Some floors need three or four coats of wax to build them up to a gloss. A good shine will hide a multitude of sins. If the floor won't shine, or it is difficult to maintain, consider replacing it or carpeting it if the lack of shine bothers you.

Pick a good-quality flooring. Remember that solid colors are tougher to maintain and keep looking good. Try to avoid the floors with grooves and indentations—they are literally the "pits." Smooth-surface floors are nicer—and much easier to keep clean.

How to Clean Carpets— For a Softer Life

10

"Never shampoo a carpet before you have to, because once you do, it will get dirty faster" (Old Wives' Tales, cont'd). That's like saying, "Never wash your socks or underwear after the first wearing, because they will get dirty faster." There are plenty of soothsayers around quoting great carpet verse and wisdom to the homemaker, most of which cost you time and money. With some simple professional techniques, you can get the job done, keep your carpets sharp, and minimize your maintenance time. My company cleans and maintains several million square feet of carpet every night. The results have produced some personal opinions, and I think what I have learned applies to household as well as commercial carpet.

Buy Quality Carpet

Most of the carpet on the market is pretty good, but remember, it costs only a few dollars more to go first class. Pay three or four dollars extra per yard to get the better grade, and have it installed professionally. It will make only a few dollars' difference in an average living room and will produce thousands of dollars of benefit in comfort, durability, enjoyment, and ease of maintenance. Personally, for homes, I love ankle-deep pile.

Selecting carpet color, style, and material is generally a personal privilege, but living with it (especially maintaining it) may not be a "privilege" if you don't choose wisely. For example, commercial carpets are so tightly woven and low-profile they are now referred to as "soft floors," not carpeted floors. Don't get too commercial-minded and buy the "wear like iron" commercial-style carpet. Believe me, it *feels* like iron when you roll around on it playing with the kids or tackle a "living room floor" project. The feel and the looks are a large part of the value of home carpeting. Much low-pile or indoor-outdoor carpet is difficult to maintain, not because it gets any dirtier than a thicker, plusher carpet, but because of its short pile and the solid colors it usually comes in. Even tiny pieces of litter or trash are highly visible on it, whereas a good thick pile or shag can tolerate, undetected, just about anything from crumbs to catcher's mitts. There's nothing wrong with letting your rug help you out a little!

A homemaker will often spend hours selecting an exact color, not realizing that the color won't stay constant for a tenth of the time the carpet is in service because of use, lighting, and depreciation. Color is one area where you should be cautious.

There is no way you can keep airborne soilants from industrial burning, street oils, home heating gases, family cooking, etc., from any carpet. All carpets will get soiled with time. Light golds, white, and light pastel flecks are wonderful and will serve you well if you live "el plusho" and your house is only a showplace. However, if you have children, grandchildren, animals, or home-study groups, those elegant light carpets will be a disaster. Light colors show the soil and are difficult to shampoo, often leaving "cow trails."

Regular Maintenance Is Important

Carpet in a home or light commercial area is easier to take care of than a hardwood floor if it is maintained properly. Its biggest problem is neglect. A carpet that looks okay is often used and abused, going unnoticed until it's too late. Then the owner of the neglected carpet says, "Huh, I wonder why the fur is all falling out?" or "I can't remember what color it used to be. It must be time to clean it." At this stage most people wake up to the fact that carpets have to be maintained. But by then it is too late. Cleanup attempts are generally futile, and the owner becomes displeased with the carpet, unjustly blaming his problems on the salesperson or manufacturer. You might think that the carpet wear and damage result only from foot traffic. Wrong! Excessive carpet damage or wear results from a combination of foot traffic, furniture "pressure," and residues (such as sand and grit) that remain in the carpet. Any sharp, abrasive particles or articles on or at the base of the carpet fibers are, as the carpet is walked on, ground against each other and in time, the fibers that aren't cut or damaged are soiled. The carpet wears out and gets soiled from the bottom as well as the top. Thus to maintain your carpet properly, you've got to keep off or remove surface litter, dust, grit, wet soils, and the old airborne soils before they are embedded in your carpet. Another reminder: Good matting will cut out a big share of this, especially wet soils and grit. Airborne dust you will have to live with. Litter you can pick up and then vacuum. The real culprit is embedded dirt. Vacuum cleaners were invented to get embedded dirt, surface dust, and litter from carpets efficiently. Few vacuums make as much impression on the carpet as they do on the user who thinks noise, chrome, and suction are the ultimate. For ages, vacuum salesmen (all equal in wind velocity to their products) have unloaded shiny, overpriced machines on customers who were fascinated by suction and attachments. Neither of these is that important in maintaining your carpet and saving yourself housecleaning hours. After showing you how a vacuum can do everything but brush your teeth, the sales approach is to lay a steel ball on the floor and suck it up into the vacuum. The gullible potential customer thinks, "If that vac-

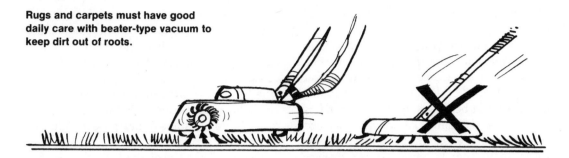

Rugs and carpets must have good daily care with beater-type vacuum to keep dirt out of roots.

uum can get a big steel ball off the carpet, sand and gravel will be a snap!"

Wrong! First, the steel ball trick is an air-flow-volume-size maneuver that any vacuum, weak or strong, old or new, can do under the right conditions. Just get a steel ball the right size for the hose or intake volume, and the "displacement" principle of vacuuming air will slurp up the ball. Now take a piece of thread and mash it into the carpet so it has a little static bind. A vacuum cleaner strong enough to pick up a piano bench will often have trouble picking up the thread because there is no "displacement lift." We've all tried to get up a thread, haven't we? Suction alone will not remove the embedded particles of dirt, grit, and sand. It will remove only the surface soil because, like the thread, the displacement lift is not there and the carpet fibers are standing in the way to effectively hold the embedded dirt, and grit, and all those other villains grinding away at your carpet. The use of a good "beater brush" vacuum is required.

Beat it! Its distinguishing feature is a rapidly rotating brush which beats, combs, and vibrates the carpet. This loosens and dislodges embedded dirt and soil so the suction can pull it up into the vacuum. Most beater brush heads are adjustable and will not wear out carpet under normal use.

Don't Abuse Your Vacuum

Eighty percent of vacuuming problems are caused not by a loose nut on the machine, but by the loose nut running it. The personality and habits of the user can take a great toll on vacuums. For example, I gave two heavy-duty commercial vacuum cleaners for Christmas in 1965, one to my mother-in-law and one to another relative. My mother-in-law's vacuum still works like new and she has used it daily for the past thirteen years. The other one lasted less than thirteen months.

The unintentional (or sometimes intentional) vacuuming of coat hangers, scout badges, apple cores, overshoes, and scissors is what hurts vacuums. That sickening knock, knock, knock you hear when the vacuum picks up one of these or similar articles generally means the blades of your turbulator fan are being sheared off. If you are vacuuming more and enjoying it less (getting up less dirt), you had probably better replace the fan. It's not uncommon to have a fine-running vacuum without suction, and a worn-out fan is generally the reason.

Note: A magnet mounted on the front of your upright machine will pick up tacks, pins, needles, scissors, can openers, or any other metal object you might miss before vacuuming. It will save injuries to crawling babies, wrestling boys, and nice, new vacuum cleaners.

Are You the One in Seven?

National studies show that one out of every seven women needs a new vacuum cleaner. If you are that one, get it before your husband spends the money on a new router

63

which he'll use once or twice during the rest of his life.

There are exceptions that might require an "exceptional" vacuum cleaner, but in 99% of the cases the market has just what you need. The ideal? I would buy two vacuums: first an upright beater-bar type. Go a step further and get a commercial upright. They are almost like the regular model sold downtown except they generally have a longer, heavier cord, a heavy-duty beater bar, a more durable turn-on switch and a better quality bag. Cloth bags are generally better: Paper filter replacement bags are costly to buy and a nuisance to store. If you use doormats efficiently, you'll cut down vacuuming intake considerably, and a cloth bag will last a long time. Cloth bags need to be emptied and shaken well to keep them from becoming impregnated with soil. If you lack a suitable alley, north forty, yard, or garage to do the airing, disposable bags might serve you better. When bags get too clogged, you'll smell "resident dust" when you click the vacuum on. Don't be alarmed until you can see it pouring out when you start the vacuum up. Then you'd better do some vigorous shaking, inside and out. An interesting

Never feel under beater vacuum to see if it is working!

exception, where paper disposables are an advantage, is in a tropical climate, where there are bugs, lizards, ants, and other creatures great and small, capable of hiding in deep shag. Their condition after passing through the beater bar and fan blades is such that a cloth bag would soon be befouled.

There are some pretty good upright vacuums on the market. In the buildings we clean professionally all over the U.S., we use Eurekas, Kirbys, Hoovers, Royals, Advance, and others. They all work fine if maintained properly. People either love or hate their vacuums beyond all reason, so I never try to switch a Kirby lover to a Eureka or a Hoover. You should be able to buy a first-class commercial upright for $150-$200.

Resist buying a boxful of attachments that do everything from sterilizing to painting. Most of them are trinket productions, and gradually the gadget accessories break or get lost and eventually the machine is only used for what you needed it for in the first place—to vacuum!

My criticism of attachments is well documented by your own experience. That big display box of nickel-plated gizmos to hook up to your vacuum is a dandy selling point, but it is shuffled, unused, from closet to closet for years until the box disintegrates or wears out. Then the tools themselves are banged around but never used. Finally, after 12 years, you need the goose-necked anteater attachment to vacuum the glove box of the car. Then you can't find it! Don't buy them. Get a sturdy, simple upright. (Do be sure to get a vacuum with a long cord—who among us has not wished a hundred times that the vacuum cord was "just ten feet longer"? Extension cords are a pain and cut your efficiency greatly. [Every time you need to use it you have to hunt it down from the family member who borrowed it for some other purpose.])

Then invest in a tank-type wet-dry vacuum. You'll be money and time ahead.

The Wet-Dry Vacuum

In addition to your upright, get a tank-type wet-dry vacuum. A wet-dry is a vacuum that will pull in both dry material and water. Generally this is accomplished by a simple filter adjustment. Wet-drys are great! They are the vacuums to buy the attachments for, and the first one should be an extra-long hose.

A five-gallon or smaller wet-dry is fine for household use. They range in price from $65 to $500. For around $275, you should be able to obtain a beautiful commercial unit which will last for years, if your neighbors or relatives don't find out. When they do, your efficient little wet-dry will be cleaning carpet spills, spots, car upholstery, floors, furniture, drapes, rafters (another reason for a long hose), carpet edges, campers, boats . . . the list could go on, take my word for it.

These two vacuums are approximately a $500 investment and will cover all your vacuum needs plus a few dozen you never thought about before.

A Vacuuming in Time . . .

A good carpet-cleaning program will free you from hours of work and emotional anguish. Clean carpets look and feel better, and they last longer. A regularly maintained carpet means less frequent shampooing, less of your time expended, and more compliments from your guests!

The ideal carpet care plan is to (1) keep all possible dust, dirt, and abrasive material from getting on the carpet—the job of good matting; (2) regularly extract all possible litter and harmful embedded debris from the carpet—the job of a good vacuum; (3) keep the surface grime off the top of the carpet so that it can't penetrate—the job of effective surface cleaning.

Vacuum carpets and mats regularly. Don't wait until you can see the dirt. Because it may be possible to camouflage crumbs, dog biscuits, pins, pennies, and peelings in a big luxurious shag doesn't mean you should overdo it. All materials detrimental to carpeting should be kept out of the carpet. I've seen homes go from 8 to 10 years before the carpets needed shampooing, all because of good matting and regular maintenance. Saving on shampooing is wise because shampooing is expensive, whether you do it yourself or have it done professionally.

Stairways are a pain, and I've found the easy way to keep stairs and corners vacuumed is a tank-type vacuum with a long hose and a small mounted upholstery tool attachment on the end of a "wand." True, there is no beater, but in this case the stronger suction from the small attachment and vigorous hand action do just as well. (Using your upright vacuum on the stairs once in a while will prevent dirt from becoming embedded.)

Always keep your vacuum on carpeted area while it is running. I've ruined a beautiful wood floor by running a low-adjusted vacuum over it. The metal part of the beater bar thumped the floor on every rotation and dented it (at great expense to me, since our insurance covers liability but not stupidity).

Take care of your vacuum regularly. It's one of your most important household tools. The biggest secret of efficient vacuuming is *keeping your vacuum well maintained.*

Spots and Stains

For spot and stain removal, I've gathered the opinions of many experts, housewives, and carpet manufacturers to contruct the following home approach. A guide to dealing with specific stains is located at the end of this chapter.

How to Remove Carpet Stains

1

Catch the spot or stain when it's fresh. Chances for removal are 75% better.

2

Carefully blot or scrape the entire stained area before applying any solution. Avoid using liquids that might spread the stain.

3

Before using any chemicals, test carpet in a small, inconspicuous area to make sure damage or discoloration won't occur.

4

Do not *rub* the spill because it might spread the problem—work spot cleaner from the outside of the stain toward the inside to avoid spreading the stain.

5

After treatment, blot all moisture up. Dry with a Turkish towel and brush the nap to a standing position after the stain is gone. Be sure you blot with a clean white (not colored) cloth.

6

After final blotting, if you feel there is still too much moisture before you brush up the nap, place a stack of white cloth towels about ¾ inch thick over the spot and weight them with a heavy object.

Soil Retardant

It is generally wise to treat carpet with soil retardant.

A soil retardant is a chemical treatment which helps carpet resist soiling and helps prevent water-and oil-based spots and spills from becoming hard-to-remove stains. Water-base soiling agents especially, such as soft drinks, milk, coffee, tea, mud, and winter slush cause big maintenance problems because they soak into carpet fibers and backing and rapidly deteriorate appearance.

Soil retardants can be applied to old or new *clean* carpeting.

The best-known brand of soil retardant is Scotchgard, made by the 3M Company. If applied correctly, it can be a real boon. After spending time in the 3M testing labs observing control blocks of carpet, treated and untreated, I was impressed. Even though this chemical may appear to be easy to apply, my suggestion is that you use recommended professional equipment and application techniques to get the best results.

Just because carpet is protected by a soil retardant doesn't mean you can relax. You must still keep up your regular schedule of carpet cleaning and maintenance. Your carpets will last much longer and look much better. Remember, when you start noticing that your carpets look bad, it's too late!

Anti-Static Agents

Static electricity is the mild shock produced when you touch a metal object after walking across a carpet. It is the result of friction. While not harmful, the shock can be irritating. And static electricity has a magnetic effect on dust particles in the air. By eliminating static, you keep your carpet cleaner. Some carpeting contains a small amount of stainless steel fiber which dissipates static electricity. For carpeting that lacks this feature, applying anti-static agents to the carpet

immediately after installation can help the problem.

All rug equipment is awkward, heavy, and requires some skill to use.

Shampooing the Carpet

If your carpets haven't had proper maintenance, and you think they are too far gone, a major cleaning, washing, or, as most call it, "shampooing," is needed. There are several ways to determine when shampooing is needed:

1.   Carpet is matted and sticky.

2.   Compare with a saved remnant of your carpet. Many carpets soil and darken so gradually you don't realize it's happening. (Remember, of course, that *every* carpet loses some color by fading, age, and daily wear and tear.)

3.   You can see a grimy circle (three-foot radius) around the TV chair.

4.   A dust storm develops when you walk across it!

You have two choices to get the job done. Do it yourself, or call a professional. I am the first to push independence and "do your own thing," but I caution you about the pitfalls of shampooing your own carpet. It is not necessarily a complicated job to do your own, but don't be deceived by the propaganda of trouble-free, money-saving, automatic, do-it-all-yourself machinery. The operator of the machine has to have some knowlege and the ability to adapt to different carpet-cleaning requirements, or else a poor cleaning job, overwetting, or fiber and backing damage will result. It amazes me that people will spend $2,500 for a carpet, then attack it with powerful cleaning gear without any experience whatsoever.

Another pitfall is cost-value miscalculations. Take, for example, a 14x20 living room carpet, which a professional might do for $28. A woman and her husband (who is missing a fishing trip) will drive 10 miles across town, rent a big steamer or rug outfit for $15. They will buy some chemicals for $5. Then they will skin up the family car getting it in and drive another 10 miles home. They'll unload the heavy equipment, grunting and groaning. Then they'll move furniture, read directions, and spend most of the Saturday cleaning carpet, and probably will have to drive back for

more shampoo. The results will be questionable.

Once they are finished, it is a repeat performance of loading and driving to return the equipment. At the end of the day, they have spent $35 on gas, rent, shampoos, etc.—not to mention their time; they are dead tired; have experienced a smashed hand, three arguments, two dog fights; and come Sunday night the carpet still isn't dry in places. I've cleaned carpets for 20 years, and always do my own because I know how and have the equipment available, but I would never do my own if I had to round up and rent the mediocre machines available and go through all that. I couldn't afford it and wouldn't enjoy the hassle.

Then again, not all so-called professionals are professionals. Some "carpet cleaners" are opportunists who were franchised and hired for a big kill; their training has been by trial-and-error rug-shrinking jobs. The method used in shampooing carpets is important. The TV demonstration of a great contrast when a little foamy carpet shampoo is rubbed on is deceptive. That isn't cleanliness you behold, but the "optical brightening" most carpets exhibit when wetted. Many carpets lightly covered with a foam job appear to gleam and sparkle. However, they can still be filthy. This has been the story with most home carpet-cleaning methods and in fact is the reason you so often hear: "Never shampoo your carpets, for once you do, they will get dirty faster." They *do* get dirty faster, but only because the surface was grazed with a dab of shampoo, and the the dirt and soap are carried by the moisture down to the bottom of the fibers, only to emerge quickly when the carpet is in use again. Also, many shampoos leave a soil-attracting residue on the carpet fibers.

You will be approached with the "mist" method, the "dry foam" method, the "liquid" method, and the latest, the "steam" method. I

Do it Yourself—
Rent $15 Cleaner $5
Car $3 Time $5
Results ?

Professional —$16.74

Carefully weigh variables involved in cleaning carpets: when, how much, and by whom?

The reason carpets soil faster after shampooing is . . . most "miracle" systems clean only the surface.

For heavily soiled carpet— Agitate with shampooer and rinse with an extractor.

If only the surface is soiled, use
1. **Light foam**
2. **Yarn bonnet**
3. **Light extraction**

wouldn't use any of these on my carpets because they are all obsolete or ineffective in some way. "Steam" is not what it is cracked up to be, but when steam cleaning hit the market, it positively revolutionized carpet cleaning. It wasn't the steam itself but the "extraction" process that was so novel. Cleaning solution is injected by force into the carpet, and a super-duper wet vacuum is used immediately to pull almost all the moisture back out. It is my opinion that steam extraction alone generally won't clean an old, dirty carpet: Rotary motion or scrubbing action with shampoo should be applied to the carpet to loosen and deep-clean it, and this should be followed by "extracting" to remove all dirt, soap, etc. Rake or sweep the carpet to a stand-up position to dry after shampooing.

The Bonnet System

One new method used with success commercially which I feel will be adopted for home use is the spin-clean, or yarn bonnet, system.

The bonnet system is a surface-cleaning procedure in which the carpet is wiped or rubbed clean with a heavy cloth "bonnet" or Turkish towel. It is not to be mistaken for a carpet deep-cleaning operation. It is a carpet-maintenance technique intended to never let carpet get into a condition of needing a major shampooing. The bonnet system is being used by most progressive commercial companies. I have been in a Bell System office in Pasadena, California, which has used this system for seven years. The carpets, even in the reception area, are clean and new-looking.

The "bonnet treatment" done twice monthly or more often in a home is fast, easy, and inexpensive. It is a good maintenance system that delays or precludes shampooing, and keeps carpets fresh and consistently clean.

The process is quite simple. Assuming you have a good daily vacuuming program, most dirt will accumulate on top of the carpet

Block legs with protection	If imprint remains—
Rub with a bit of clear water—	Brush up and let dry.

rather than being transferred to the roots. A simple yarn disc or pad, two inches or so thick, is moistened with a carpet-cleaning solution and wrung in your roller mop bucket. Then it is mounted under a buffer (household floor polisher) and run over the carpet. The bonnet will pick up and absorb surface grime and soils. The floor "buffer" spins in a rotating motion on the carpet. When the cloth becomes dirty, it is turned over and the process is repeated. When both sides are dirty, rinse the bonnet clean in the mop bucket, wring, and repeat.

For heavy-use areas like commercial offices, a three-times-a-week application might be necessary; in a home, twice a month would be just right. It does take a certain solution like Argo Sheen to produce best results, so check with a professional supplier if you plan to try the bonnet system. A janitorial supply house can direct you to the right chemical to clean with and a bonnet to fit your floor machine.

Although this is not presently a well-known system, it will be, and small oscillating (like Square Buff) or rotary machines will be feasible to own. Most "household gimmick" machines aren't as fast and effective as a good commercial unit. Four or five neighbors or relatives might go in together on a pass-around unit. I like the bonnet system because it holds carpets to a consistent level of cleanliness and replaces the old inefficient up-and-down approach to cleaning. There is also something spiritually uplifting about a clean fresh expanse of carpet.

Simple hanger protects drapes from damage during carpet cleaning.

Coping with Carpet Catastrophes

Carpet problems (spills, burns, spots, etc.) are a reality in the home just as they are in the commercial buildings I clean. A puddle of orange pop on your living room rug will upset you just as surely as a glaring coffee stain on the carpeting in front of a bank teller will turn off customers. A few basic maneuvers can solve most of these problems (not all, because sometimes a stain is a *stain*), and you can do them as well as (probably better than) a professional.

Basic Tools and Supplies

Keep the following items on hand to attack fresh spills on your carpets:

- **Neutral detergent,** i.e., one that is advertised as safe for fine fabrics, such as Trend, Vel, Dreft, or Ivory Liquid. Dilute 20:1 with water to use for spot removal.
- **Common household ammonia**—clear, sudsy, or lemon-scented. When using ammonia for spot removal, always dilute with 10 parts water.
- **Nonflammable dry-cleaning fluid,** such as Carbona, Renuzit, Energine, or "perk" (perchloroethylene, used by professional dry cleaners). Use straight from the container. *Do not* use gasoline, lighter fluid, or carbon tetrachloride.
- **Distilled white vinegar.** Dilute 50-50 with water.
- **Clean white terry cloth towels.**
- **A soft-bristled scrub brush.**
- **A spatula or putty knife.**
- **A wet-dry vacuum.**

Note: Try to avoid wet cleaning on wool. Use dry-cleaning solvents whenever possible.

Remember

Keep cleaning solutions and tools out of reach of little children, for their safety. I would suggest you store your spot removal tools and supplies in a small plastic hand carrying tray or "maid basket." This will hold and organize your supplies safely for quick attack on spots.

STAIN/SPOT	COMPOSITION	METHOD
acids (bowl cleaner, drain cleaner, vinegar)	hydrochloric, acetic, and other acids	Apply a solution of baking soda and water until, by feel and smell, spot has disappeared. Then apply ammonia solution and rinse with cold water.
alcoholic beverages	alcohol, sugar, tannin, coloring	Apply detergent solution; blot. Apply vinegar solution; blot. Apply ammonia solution; blot. Bleach with 3-5% hydrogen peroxide or sodium perborate if necessary. Rinse with cold water; blot dry.

alkali (lye, concentrated ammonia, TSP—trisodium phosphate)	strong alkaline compounds	Apply vinegar solution, then rinse and blot.
butter, margarine	vegetable dye, milk, salt, preservatives, vegetable and animal fats and oils	Apply dry-cleaning solvent; blot. Apply detergent solution; blot dry. Rinse; blot dry.
blood	albumin, fat, fibrin, iron	Scrape off surface. Apply cool detergent solution; blot. Apply cool ammonia solution; blot. Rinse; blot dry. Apply rust remover followed by 3-5% hydrogen peroxide if stain remains.
candle wax	petroleum, animal and vegetable fats and oils; basic dyes	Scrape off surface. Apply dry-cleaning solvent; blot. Repeat.
catsup, tomato sauce	tomatoes, salt, sugar, spices, tannin, vinegar, onions	Apply cool detergent or ammonia solution; blot. If stain remains, apply 3-5% hydrogen peroxide. Rinse; blot dry.
chewing gum	resins, sugar	If hard and solid, apply commercial aerosol gum freeze (ice cubes in a plastic bag will work sometimes) until the gum is brittle. Break into pieces and vacuum up. Apply dry-cleaning solvent to residue.
chocolate	oil, grease, cocoa, butter, coloring, sugar, milk	Scrape off surface. Apply cool detergent solution; blot. Apply ammonia solution; blot. Apply vinegar solution; blot. Rinse; blot dry.
cigarette burns	melted fibers (or worse—a hole!)	If the burn is slight, rub with dry steel wool, or, if you feel confident, trim the tufts. If the burn is bad, have a professional "doughnut cut" the damaged area and plug a new piece in, or do it yourself.
coffee	tannin, sugar	Rub with a paste of raw egg yolk; rinse. If stain is old, apply a few drops of denatured alcohol; rinse.

crayon	wax, grease, pigments	Apply dry-cleaning solvent; blot. Apply detergent solution. Rinse; blot dry.
food coloring/dyes	artificial food colors, propylene-glycol	Apply detergent solution, blotting frequently (a dried stain can easily spread when wet). Repeat until towel picks up no color. Apply ammonia solution; blot. Rinse; blot dry.
furniture polish with "scratch cover," wood stain	petroleum distillate, oils, pigments	Apply dry-cleaning solvent; blot. Apply detergent solution; blot. Rinse; blot dry. (This stain is almost impossible to remove completely if you don't catch it while fresh, so use a better dropcloth next time or do it in the basement or garage.)
grass stains	tannin, acids, oils, chlorophyll	Apply amyl acetate, if available, to remove chlorophyll; blot. Apply detergent solution; blot. Rinse; blot. Apply ammonia solution; blot. Apply vinegar solution; blot. Rinse; blot dry. If necessary, apply 3-5% hydrogen peroxide; use caution.
grease, oil	petroleum derivatives	Apply paint thinner or perk. Work to center to avoid ring. Blot. Apply light detergent solution; rinse.
ink (ballpoint)	basic or soluble aniline dyes, insoluble organic solvents, oils, resins, gums, binding agents such as shellac, varnish, or petroleum	Apply dry-cleaning solvent; blot. Apply denatured alcohol; blot. Apply amyl acetate if available, or acetone (nail polish remover, but *don't* use it on acetate fibers!). If stain remains, apply rust remover or oxalic acid solution. Professional plugging or bleaching may be necessary.
ink (India)	pigment dispersed in water with a binder	Apply dry-cleaning solvent. Apply detergent solution; blot. Apply ammonia solution; blot. Rinse; blot dry. (This stain is often permanent and the spot may have to be plugged.)
iodine, mercurochrome, merthiolate	alcohol, iodine, mercury compounds	Apply denatured alcohol; blot. Apply ammonia solution; blot. Rinse. (Some stain may remain.)

jam, jelly	fruit pulp, sugar, tannin, preservatives	Apply detergent solution; blot. Apply vinegar solution; blot. Rinse; blot dry.
lipstick	pigment or dye in fat, waxes, and oils	Scrape off surface, taking care not to spread the stain. Apply dry-cleaning solvent; blot. Apply detergent solution; blot. Apply ammonia solution; blot. Apply vinegar solution; blot. Rinse; blot.
mildew	grayish or brownish spots or splotches produced by fungus	Apply solution of one teaspoon disinfectant cleaner to one cup water; blot. Apply ammonia solution; blot. Rinse; blot. Keep area dry!
milk, cream, ice cream	sugar, butterfat, coloring and flavoring agents	Apply ammonia solution; rinse. If area is large, shampoo afterward.
mud	soil with greases and oils, clay, iron	Allow to dry and brush or scrape off as much as possible. Apply detergent or ammonia solution; blot. Rinse; blot dry. If stain remains, apply dry-cleaning solvent; blot dry.
mustard	mustard seed, vinegar, salt, spices, oils	Apply detergent solution; blot. Apply vinegar solution; blot. If stain remains, apply rust remover or hydrogen peroxide solution; blot. Do not use ammonia or alkalies.
nail polish	dye or pigment in liquid cellulose acetate base, solvent, plasticizer	Apply dry-cleaning solvent. Apply amyl acetate, if available, acetone or nail polish remover—*test first*. If stain remains, apply detergent solution; blot dry. Apply ammonia solution; blot. Apply vinegar solution; blot. Rinse; blot dry.
odors	airborne particles emanating from organic matter in the carpet	Apply solution of one teaspoon disinfectant cleaner to one cup water. Follow with water-soluble deodorant. If an odor has permeated the carpet *and* the backing or mat, it is nearly impossible to get out. Ask a reliable carpet cleaner what they use or have them do it for you.

paint (oil base)	pigments, drying oils, resins, gums, volatile solvents	Check label on paint for specific thinner or solvent to use, or apply dry-cleaning solvent. If stain remains, cover it with towels dampened with dry-cleaning solvent or paint thinner to soften for several hours; blot with solvent. Apply several drops of detergent solution and work into the stain; blot. Apply ammonia solution; blot. Rinse with warm water; blot dry.
paint (water base)	water, latex, pigments, emulsifiers, preservatives	Apply detergent solution; blot. Apply ammonia solution; blot. Rinse; blot. If a paint spill is dried, a little lacquer thinner will soften and remove. (It could also melt the carpet, so test first.)
rust	iron oxide	Rub with steel wool, then apply commercial rust remover if necessary.
shoe polish	waxes, resins, solvents, dyes, shellac, alcohol, tannin	Apply dry-cleaning solvent. Apply detergent solution; blot. Apply ammonia solution; blot. Rinse; blot dry. If stain remains, bleaching with 3-5% hydrogen peroxide or professional plugging may be necessary.
urine	urea, uric acid, ammonia, organic acids, pigments, cholesterol, albumins, proteoses	Blot up as much as possible. Apply detergent solution, then ammonia solution; blot. Apply vinegar solution; blot. Rinse; blot dry. If stain remains, apply rust remover or oxalic acid solution; bleaching with 3-5% hydrogen peroxide or sodium perborate might be necessary. (Urine stains may remove dye from fibers.)
vomit	food, mucus, albumins, acids	Blot up as much as possible. Apply detergent solution; blot. Apply ammonia solution; blot. Apply vinegar solution; blot. Rinse; blot dry.

For spots not listed, match them up to those with a similar composition and use a similar approach. Upholstery can be treated in much the same way as carpet. Remember to follow the six steps:
1. Catch it fast.
2. Blot or scrape.
3. Test (go at it easy).
4. Work to center.
5. Soak up or blot—don't rub.
6. Absorb.
Be patient—give the chemicals time to work. Don't expect all stains to come out immediately—most take some time.

Bleaching is a last resort, and I don't generally recommend it, unless you want a little adventure or a new conversation piece (spot).

Most old stains and spots can't be removed, so don't get your hopes up too high about that three-year-old cherry popsicle stain you've had the lamp table over. It might have to remain until you replace the rug!

What to Do About Furniture ¹¹

"What should I do about furniture?" is a question I'm asked repeatedly by home-makers. As a male, my attitude toward furniture is, "I dislike moving it, and I dislike buying it even more." A woman has a finer apprecia-tion for furniture because she is often the one who chooses it. And much of her time is spent maintaining it and caring for its appearance.

In an attempt to eliminate both of my furniture frustrations, I designed most of the furniture out of a home we built in the resort mountains of Sun Valley, Idaho. Our living room had an octagonal conversation pit pad-ded with vinyl-backed cushions. Twelve or thir-teen people could sit and visit comfortably. A two-stair landing faced into the living room area and ten or twelve more visitors could sit on plush padded stairs looking into the living room. This house didn't have a single piece of furniture except for the beds and the dining room set. I built the stereo and bookcases in, to eliminate cabinets and stands. Beds were built to the floor and other such technical adjustments were made to eliminate the clutter and upkeep of furniture. Our home was beautiful and usable for family and youth groups of up to 40, and I didn't have to buy furniture or move it!

But for most of you, furniture not only must be bought and moved, it must be cleaned. So the question becomes, "How do I keep my furniture looking nice without a lot of time and effort?"

Attempts to answer this question have greatly stimulated the sales of "miracle" furniture polishes. Think about the message given by thousands of TV furniture polish commercials: "fast and easy"; "polished clean and lint-free"; "see yourself reflected"; "Brand X shines your dingy furniture better than Grandma's beeswax and turpentine and it smells woody, lemony, and expensive." Furniture care is not that simple.

There are some ways to cut the time spent caring for furniture and make it last longer. Notice I said "ways," not "way." It isn't done with a squirt of magic aerosol furniture polish as a TV or magazine ad might suggest.

My approach to furniture cleaning is more preventive than maintenance-oriented. Buy high-quality furniture—expensive, well-manufactured furniture costs less to maintain than "el cheapo" stuff. Cheap furniture loses its crisp, elegant look rapidly and becomes conspicuously dull and shabby-looking. Once in this decrepit condition, it takes a lot of time and supplies to maintain it. And it rarely looks any better cleaned and polished than it did before you started. Select carefully and get good quality. Paying a little more cash will save a lot of your most precious commodity, personal time.

Choosing Furniture with an Eye to Cleanability

The design and style of furniture you choose will determine how many hours per day, week, or year you will have to give to maintaining it. Elaborate hand carving with lines and grooves bordered by silk, velvet, and lace and topped with stained glass is going to take more time and material to keep looking good. You are the sole judge on this one. If the prestige or decor of your home calls for the elaborate unit, *you* have to decide the long-range value of owning it. No matter what you decide, check the furniture and make sure all the surfaces can be maintained. The wood should have a finish—not just an oiled surface or a colored stain, but a *membrane finish* to prevent dirt and cleaning materials from penetrating into the wood. Lighter wood furniture shows dust less, is easier to make look good, and remains that way longer than darker furniture. Natural or bare wood that needs constant "feeding" or oiling is a pain to maintain, and, in my opinion, looks shabby in a short period of time.

Metal should have a smooth finish that is not pitted or engraved. It should be coated with baked or other hard-surface coating. Stainless steel and chrome are durable, but require a lot of effort to keep clean and bright.

Is it cleanable?   Fabric will generally be the most used and abused part of furniture. Spillage on furniture is as common as on carpet, believe it or not. Some fabric, basketry, and woven twines look superb, but grease stains and other marks on them can never be removed.

Is it restorable?   Some fabrics look great when cleaned or new but after a few people sit on them, they become tangled and matted. You've all seen velvet or fur-type material after it has been sat on. The user's rump print remains, and you have better things to do than go around brushing up the cushions to make them look good. Pick a fabric that "restores," or comes back to life, after use. Select a hard-finish fabric for dining room chairs that are used constantly. White or light-colored fabrics (especially solid colors) show and accent every spot. Fabrics with some color blend or a pattern hide dirt better. Again, this is matter of taste—but try to make it easy on yourself. Remember, furniture exists for your use and comfort.

Soil retardant. Although I question the value of some soil retardants on some carpet, I don't question it on upholstered furniture. Scotchgard (a 3M trade name), which you can buy and apply, is a lifesaver for most upholstery and for you personally. It is an excellent protection for most fabrics, making them more maintainable.

Keeping Furniture Looking Nice

Convinced that the secret of furniture maintenance is in the bottle or can of polish, the majority of us use too much of it. We build up layers of gunk which result in more work and faster surface deterioration. A treated cloth that leaves no oil or residue, yet picks up dust, is the best way to go. Throw away your feather dusters. They are the least effective. You can purchase paper dustcloths at your local janitorial supply house. They are called Massilon cloths, and they last and last. Then you can throw them away.

The pro approach might give you new ideas about furniture cleaning. We clean thousands of desktops, tabletops, chairs, stands, racks, and cabinets every night throughout the U.S. In most of our cleaning, we wipe with treated cloths to remove dust. When fingermarks have to be removed, we use a light spray of neutral cleaner or a water-damp cloth to wipe and dry-buff to a natural sheen. We avoid using polish where the finish can maintain its own luster.

When you need to polish, select one type of polish (choose one with a low-sheen gloss) and use it consistently. The reason for this is simple. Often your furniture surfaces will

come out dull and streaked because your new polish is not compatible with the old polish.

Select your polish on these merits:

1. Ease of application

2. Lastingness of protection

3. Non-smearing and -streaking

4. Safety (you want a polish that's safe for your furniture surfaces—and for you to work with)

5. Pleasing scent

6. Easy buffing

7. Ability to hide superficial scratches and blemishes

Types of Polish

Liquid or paste solvent. Hard to apply. Excellent water and abrasion resistance. Low gloss, but durable.

Clear oil polishes. Mineral oil, vegetable oil, turpentine blend used to "feed" wood. Use on bare wood and sealed wood. Has high gloss, but leaves a greasy film that collects dust and fingerprints.

Oil emulsion polishes. Cream type. Good cleaning properties, but same drawbacks as clear oil.

Water or oil wax emulsion (aerosol or spray). Contains all components needed in a good polish: protects, enhances the beauty, and is easy to dust.

Cleaning Fabric Upholstery

This is commonly referred to as "shampooing furniture." To remove stains on clean upholstery, apply the same principles you do with carpet (see Chapter 10). A surface spot can be wiped or cleaned with an applicator dampened with cleaning solution and dried with a dry, absorbent cloth. If the fabric is thoroughly soiled, it should be washed with an upholstery cleaning solution or shampoo, then rinsed out. This is where problems arise in a do-it-yourself upholstery cleaning job. Cleaning solution is scrubbed on the dirt and the upholstery fabric seems to be cleaner. Actually the surface dirt has been loosened and has sunk deeper into the fabric, along with the cleaning solution. The fabric appears clean, but it isn't. The fabric is soaked with chemical, which leaves it sticky and matted down. Get dirt and moisture out with an upholstery extractor attachment, or even a good wet-dry vacuum. Soon after the cleaning application, rinse with clear water. Spotting kits are available with professional instructions from most large carpet distributors or a janitorial supply house.

Always be sure to check manufacturers' cleaning instructions.

12
Reaching the High Places

If heights make you shake in your boots, find a daredevil and bake him some cookies. Let him climb to clean off a flyspeck, change a light bulb, paint or wash the ceiling. One of my customers had a husband full of ambition and desire to clean, but he was terrified of high places. She would hire me to wash all the high areas, saving the low stuff for his cleaning enthusiasm. One year while doing his low section, he was on a plank just six feet off the floor and caught the phobia. He lay down on the plank, dug his whitened fingernails into the wood of the plank, and froze there. His wife, unable to talk him down from the dizzying six-foot height, ended up calling the fire department (siren and all!). They finally dislodged the husband's death grip on the plank and got him onto floor level safely, but he was never sound enough emotionally to assist in cleaning again.

Be sure to adjust or limit the reaching of tall areas to fit your resources, age, nerves (and your helpers' bravery!). But don't be buffaloed by hard-to-reach areas. "Once I got going, it only took me ten minutes" is the wail of many "end-of-the-day" housekeepers. The many hours spent to get going is the bane of cleaning in high places. Access contributes greatly to success in such cleaning, yet the old shaky ladder and step stool are about the extent of most homes' scaffolding. More energy, time, and emotion are used going up and down the ladder or stool than actually doing the job at hand. And all of our effort, worry, tool procurement and arrangement seems to be focused on the few minutes we'll actually be performing the job, instead of trying to save the hours getting in position or location to start it.

As a professional housecleaner, I too have to weigh the same factors a housewife does. The equipment needed to get at the work has to be light enough to be manageable, and small enough to fit in tight areas and keep from scratching walls and woodwork. It must be *sturdy* and *safe* enough to ensure no falls. The basics 25 years of housecleaning have taught me to use are:

A Good Ladder

A plain old common ladder is one of the best all-around tools. It is versatile, manageable, and safe . . . if you select an appropriate model. For household use, the perfect stepladder size is five feet high. I have found that four-foot ladders are too short to reach and work on an eight-foot ceiling. A six-foot

ladder is too high. It nicks up the house when you carry it around. A five-foot ladder is just right for most household cleaning operations. Instead of buying several creaky wooden ladders for $20 each during your lifetime, buy a five-foot heavy-duty commercial aluminum ladder for $50 or so. You'll never regret it. It is strong and safe to use anywhere, and it will probably outlast you, even counting the 10 years it may add to your life. It can be used outside on rough terrain, and bad weather or dry storage won't hurt it.

For higher reaches every household should have a "tall" ladder, and I feel the perfect one for this purpose is an 18-foot, two-piece extension ladder. It will reduce to 10 feet for storage in the laundry room or inside the stairwell and lengthen out safely to 16 feet—enough to get the cat out of the tree, fix the aerial, or paint the trim every five years.

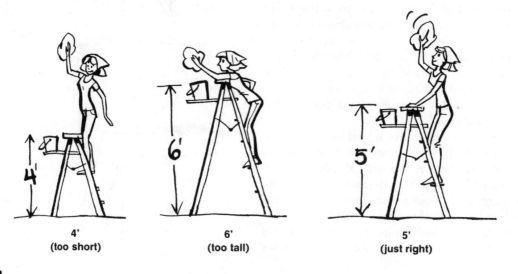

4'
(too short)

6'
(too tall)

5'
(just right)

12'

3'

Aluminum is lighter, but in an extension ladder for home use, I prefer wood or fiberglass for strength, safety, and electrical protection. Don't paint wooden ladders—paint hides breaks, cracks, and flaws and is slippery when wet. Boiled linseed oil is best for maintaining wooden ladders.

Make Yourself a Box

The harmless-looking "bench" is often used. It has a narrow base and a deceptively sturdy top. But it's too unbalanced and risky to use as a standing or cleaning tool. To replace the old bench, which has battered many a body, a simply constructed box of ¾-inch plywood is inexpensive and far superior. I'd suggest dimensions of 15x20x28 inches (see next page). Bell system has a similar unit they have used safely and effectively for years. It is called a "three-position stool." Laid flat on its side or end, it gives you three low heights to work from. Hand holes can be cut in the box's side to move it or use it for storage when it is not in use. It can also serve as a baby crib, or an extra chair when company comes.

Walk the Plank for Safety

The last and most useful tool to conquer the unreachable places is a sturdy, ordinary 2x12" plank 8 to 10 feet long. Purchase it at a lumberyard and make sure it has no loose knots, cracks, or weak areas. Redwood is good because it is light, and water seldom affects it. Sand off the corners and rough edges for handling, and it is ready to use. Don't paint or varnish it, because when it is wet or soapy, it will become slippery. The idea is to combine the stepladder, regular ladder, box, and plank whenever possible to keep you at your working area with the minimum of

Directions for the construction of your own Housecleaning Box

(You can make it a little larger or a little smaller to custom-fit you.)

Materials needed:
1 sheet of ¾" exterior plywood
1 pound of No. 8 finish nails
1 small bottle of white glue
sandpaper
1 pint of clear varnish (or
polyurethane)

Just lay out the following plan and
assemble per directions. If your
husband has traded in his $300 power
saw to buy you a new vacuum, no
sweat—a $20 saber saw will work fine!

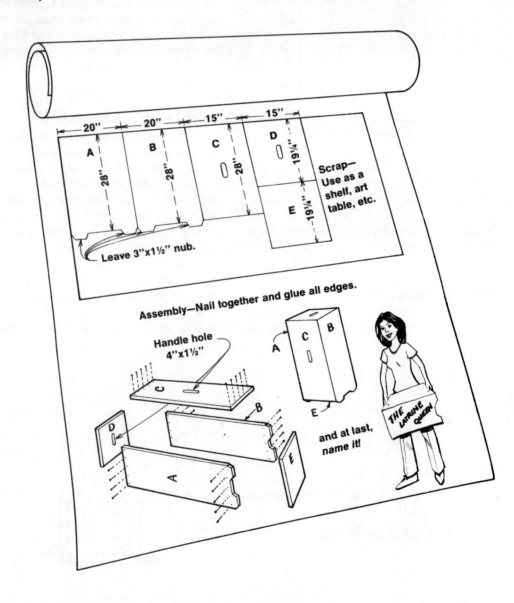

84

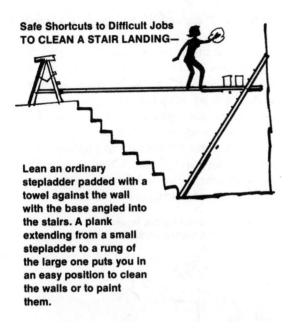

**Safe Shortcuts to Difficult Jobs
TO CLEAN A STAIR LANDING—**

Lean an ordinary stepladder padded with a towel against the wall with the base angled into the stairs. A plank extending from a small stepladder to a rung of the large one puts you in an easy position to clean the walls or to paint them.

footsteps. If you need to reach higher areas than can be reached with this combination, rent the necessary equipment, because you will seldom use it around the house.

A plank, though it may be scary to you at first, is a safe area on which to work if you are reasonably awake. The slight spongy "give" you will feel on the plank is easy to adapt to. Planks were only fatal to blindfolded pirates when they had to walk off the end. Looking up at the ceiling and moving toward the box end of the plank puts you in the same circumstance as the pirates. Always keep an extra sponge or empty bucket at the end of the plank so a nudge of the toe reminds you to stop walking. (This is a case where "kicking the bucket" is advisable for longevity.) The plank-and-ladder combination is especially effective to use on high stairwells. On stair landings and other open areas, you can figure a combination (such as the one above). It will make you love yourself for your brilliance.

The basic reason for working from a plank or ladder is safety in reaching tall areas. Most of the time, doing ceilings in a house from a ladder, you are only two feet off the floor. When in a stairwell, you are higher over the stairs, but with walls two feet on both sides of you and with a ladder at both ends, there is little risk of falls. I've seen 20 ladder accidents for every plank accident. Regular ladders must be tilted at the proper angle to keep from slipping down or tumbling over. One foot out from the base of the wall for every four feet up is just right. Keep your cleaning solution, tools, paint, and other working materials with you as much as possible. Ascending or descending a ladder or a plank for every dip depletes strength, wastes time, and exposes you more often to mishap.

Keep Your Working Stuff Near You!

I've heard claims that a woman walks 8 to 15 miles a day doing housework. I wouldn't doubt it. I used to walk one mile per room I cleaned until I learned to keep my cleaning tools within reach. Too many people place their tools and buckets in a central "cleaning station" in the room and walk three, four, or even five or six steps back and forth constantly during a project. They spend 50% of their time and energy traveling. If you need the exercise, continue to use a central cleaning station. If you want to get the job done and have energy left for a tennis game, bowling, or other personal sporting around, figure how to keep your tools (sponges, buckets, cloths, screwdriver, etc.) within your reach. (For example, if you are washing cupboards, set tools on the counter instead of on the floor—same with painting.) If you hang the bucket on the ladder or hold it in your hand, it will save the bend and dip all the way to the floor and back up. Try it—you'll be amazed at the time and effort you save!

A trick I've tried without much success is moving a folding stepladder without moving

of the best "under-$20" investments you will ever make.

A cleaning towel (see Chapter 13) slipped over each end of the ladder will keep it from marking up your walls. A dry sponge under each leg will prevent it from slipping if the surface the legs rest on is questionable. Tennis shoes are great to clean in.

A final word of advice: Put your name on your ladders and planks. When your neighbors spot them, they will want to try out your new system of reaching high places.

Don't try this if you don't want to risk a broken neck.

the buckets or tools. I bat about 60%. The other 40% has cost me wet carpets, skinned shins, painted faces, and starting over again. It is also extremely risky to tie or lay the plank on planters, metal railings, fireplace mantels, or other trim. Most of these were designed to be looked at, not to support 150 pounds or more of plank, solutions, and person. Mortar is not stout. It spaces rocks and bricks for compressed strength, but not tensile strength. Place ladders on supports where strength is sure. When you've finished your cleaning job, the two ladders can be stored in a small area. You'll use the plank for many things. It is one

Simplified Wall and Ceiling Cleaning

13

I once bid to wash walls in six large offices, a long hall, lobby, entrances, and storage areas in a Massey-Ferguson tractor dealer's office. I was the low bid at the price of $275. Our new crew was busy on the scheduled day, so I tackled the job alone. Seven hours later, I had it finished and more than a few compliments on the quality of the job. On another occasion, I washed all the walls, ceilings, and woodwork in a three-bedroom modern home in less than one day—alone. I'm no more a "super" wall and ceiling cleaner than you are. In fact, I'm certain that many of you could keep up with me or beat me on my best day, if you'd use the same approach I did.

There are two reasons why wall and ceiling cleaning will become one of your favorite housecleaning tasks when you do it my way: (1) It is easy and trouble-free and (2) The delight of seeing the surface come clean is great! In fact, you are going to find washing your walls and ceilings so easy and satisfying, you'll want to wash your friends' walls and ceilings just to show off. Your days of struggling with a half-filled bucket of grimy wall-washing solution will end as you finish this chapter, if you follow the simple principles it sets forth.

We outlined the basic principle of cleaning in Chapter 6, so now for the technique and tools of wall cleaning. Your height, your arm strength, or the degree of dirt accumulated doesn't make much difference in the time and effort it takes to clean walls and ceilings.

Using your head and the right tools *will* make a difference. One of the first and most important (and least known) tools of housecleaning is a chemically treated rubber sponge called a *dry sponge*. I know all of you have seen them. They are impregnated with some secret formula that makes the sponge super-absorbent and gently abrasive for removing dirt. Dry sponges are generally tan or red in color and come on handles, or as flat 7x6x½-inch pads. The pad is by far the best way to go because it has a larger number of usable surfaces. Dry sponges come wrapped in cellophane to keep the embedded chemical fresh. When you unwrap them, they will feel dry and spongy. Never, never use water on them or get them wet (not a drop)—or they will become useless for cleaning. Most people use dry sponges for cleaning wallpaper. (Now more of you will know what I am referring to.) They are excellent on wallpaper, much better than "dough" wallpaper cleaners that crumble and stick!

On white ceiling acoustic tile and on most flat oil- or latex-painted walls, one swipe of a dry sponge will remove the dirt. It will not remove fingerprints or flyspecks—only the film of dirt. In most homes, dry-sponging the ceiling will leave it perfect. I've washed behind a dry sponge several times, not believing that the sponge could get all the dirt out, but it did—every bit of it! In fact, on some porous walls or painted surfaces where the dirt is embedded deeply a dry sponge is superior to washing. Even on walls that are smoke-damaged, ten minutes of dry-sponging the room prior to washing will reduce washing time and expense more than 50%. When dry-sponging, you don't have to stop to dip or rinse. Just get to the surface and swipe in four-foot lengths (or shorter if your arms are shorter). The sponge will absorb the dirt and begin to get black. It will hold the dirt as you clean along, but soon its saturation point is reached and you must switch the surface area of the sponge and keep going. The residue that falls from the sponge won't stain or stick, and it is easily vacuumed up after the job is done.

Each pad-type sponge has eight good surfaces, if used correctly. The handled or the square-type dry sponges are great, except once their surface is saturated, the whole sponge is no longer usable. When the sponge is black on both sides, throw it away. Washing them doesn't work. Dry sponges cost a little over a dollar and are worth ten times that for the job they do and the time they save.

The proper way to hold a dry sponge is illustrated here:

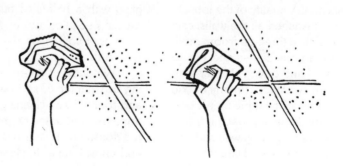

A dry sponge won't clean enamel or greasy surfaces, so don't be disappointed when you make a swipe across the kitchen or bathroom wall and nothing radical happens.

If you go into the bedroom and make a swipe across the ceiling and can't see where you have just been, the ceiling doesn't need cleaning and the walls probably don't either. Just clean the light fixtures, the fingerprints, the woodwork, and take off the rest of the hour you allowed for bedroom cleaning. Once the dry-sponging is out of the way, the remaining areas, not cleaned with a dry sponge, will have to be washed. This can be accomplished rather simply if the right tools and methods are used.

Your Rag Is Your Worst Enemy

There is no question that the most famous household cleaning tool is the simple little item known as a "rag." Your rags have been salvaged from ancient sheets, tattered diapers, worn-out T-shirts, flour sacks, and other fabric scraps. Using a rag to clean with is like using a rake to comb your hair: rather ineffective. For 500 years cloth designers have been working to develop fabrics that repel liquids and stains. They've succeeded, and we have scores of fabrics today that resist moisture—which makes them terrible for cleaning. Yet we can't seem to resist saving trouser legs, old slips, and a thousand other unsuitable fabrics for cleaning rags. *Don't do it!* "Kimbees" are for kids, not kitchen ceilings. I'm certain that one thing that makes the professional a three times faster—and better—cleaner than the homemaker is the fact that homemakers are hung up on rags. Rags are only good for paint cleanup, stuffing rag dolls, blowing your nose, or signaling surrender when the cleaning gets you down. Henceforth, the term "rag" must be banished from your housecleaning vocabulary and from your basket of cleaning tools. The "rag" in your housecleaning tool bag will be replaced with an item called a "cleaning cloth."

The Noble Cleaning Cloth

A cleaning cloth is made from a salvaged or new heavy Turkish (cotton terry cloth) towel. I've had a lot of questions as to what kind of toweling to use. The big worry is that the new poly/cotton blends are not as absorbent as the old pure cotton towels. *Not so!* They are an improvement! The polyester is used for the base fabric and the cotton to make the pile (nibbers). Moisture rarely gets to the base anyway, and the polyester dries faster and resists wrinkles. (A wrinkle-resistant cleaning cloth—now *that's* class!) But do be sure to use toweling with high cotton content.

First cut the towel into an 18x18-inch flat piece, then fold it over and sew the one long side, leaving it like a tube, open on both ends. Be sure to hem the edge by folding it twice. You have a hand-sized surface of thick absorbent terry cloth to efficiently cover every inch of surface it passes over. It is not like the old linen bedsheet that just streaks and smears the film around. (We wouldn't think of drying *ourselves* on a piece of sheet after a bath.)

If you refold your cleaning towels right and use both sides, you have eight efficient surfaces to use; turn the towel inside out and you have eight more. Sixteen surfaces on one little cleaning cloth! They are 50% more efficient and safer than rags. (Terry cleaning cloths are great to protect the hands from scrapes, cuts, and ripped fingernails.) I often clean an entire large bedroom using only three cleaning cloths. When you are finished and the cleaning cloths are damp and dirty, throw them in the washer.

Soiled cleaning cloths are simply washed and tumble-dried for reuse.

You don't have to use much soap, because the towels will be full of the cleaner you've been using. The towels will come out as clean as they were before you used them. Don't hang them on the line or they will be stiff as a board and impossible to use the next time: Be sure to tumble-dry them! Twenty pads will clean your entire house and, if washed and stored properly, will last for years. If you use the towels a little drier, the sheens and streaks you often see on kitchen walls or other glossy enameled areas will be polished off as you wash along.

Your Basic Cleaning Tools

The dry sponge and cleaning cloth are the main "professional" tools you need to do most housecleaning, so don't prepare yourself a long list of material and equipment. The rest of the items you probably already have around the house, so round them up: one empty bucket, one bucket half full of warm water, an ordinary cellulose sponge (that fits your hand), and a jug of your favorite cleaner (mine is ammonia). That's it!

(I know what you are thinking now. "Man, wouldn't a two-compartment bucket be great!" No . . . it wouldn't. They are, without question, one of the most worthless instruments ever palmed off on a housecleaner. Take my word for it.)

Mix your cleaning solution following directions on the container. Make sure your cleaning compound is one capable of cutting the dirt you want to remove. Ammonia or good commercial neutral cleaner concentrates will be fine unless you are dealing with an extremely grease-laden kitchen, where a little ammoniated wax stripper or degreaser added to the solution will make the job much easier.

Before beginning, reinforce your attitude. I've read books and articles on cleaning house which say, "Allow yourself a day to a week for each room." You are going to clean it, not rebuild it! Allow yourself a couple of hours (maybe three if you anticipate being interrupted). Prolonging a simple job will wear down your initiative and determination.

4 Basic items Are Needed

A bucket of warm water with ammonia or neutral cleaner   An empty bucket   A sponge   A cleaning cloth (has 8 cleaning surfaces)   . . . and a dirty wall

Cleaning procedure: You have your ladder or scaffolding in position, and now you are ready to begin! Your solution should be where you don't have to climb 30 feet to dip your sponge. Placing your solution, or cleaning water, in the right place is extremely important. ALWAYS KEEP IT AS CLOSE TO YOUR WORKING AREA AS POSSIBLE. Spilling solution was one of my major problems in my beginning housecleaning days. I finally learned to set the bucket next to me, not in back of me, on a table, or in the middle of the floor. Set it in a visible spot. The most common spillage problems are tripping over buckets or moving a piece of furniture, behind which a full bucket of solution is hidden. If you do spill, run for the wet-dry vacuum and get all the moisture out you can. Then rinse with clear water to get the ammonia (or other cleaning agent) out. Again, remember to fill your buckets only half full (if you fill them to the brim they will be top-heavy and can easily

**Keep bucket close to
the wall—**

NOT at your feet!

**Dip sponge ¼ inch into cleaning
solution. Wet an area about 3' square.**

spill), and keep the dirty bucket dumped in the toilet regularly (after each room), for if it spills you will have a tough cleanup problem.

Take a damp sponge and dip it in the solution ¼ inch (not all the way in). This will give you plenty of cleaning solution to wet the wall or ceiling and leave the remaining thickness of the sponge dry enough to absorb any water which otherwise would run down your arms or splash into your eyes.

I know all the books say to start at the bottom of the wall and work up, because if you dribble on the lower unwashed wall from the top, it might stain: an old wives' tale. I never do it! In extreme cases with old paints and spectacularly dirty walls, it might be wise, but to me, it is discouraging to start at the bottom, get it clean, then get to the top and dribble on the clean wall. I can't stand to back up and redo an area I have already done. So I start at the top and recommend that you do the same.

How large an area you work on at one time depends, of course, on (1) your reach; (2) how soiled the surface is; and (3) how fast the solution will dry on the surface. A 3x3-foot section is just about right for the average person. Quickly cover the whole area with the solution on the sponge. Do not press hard or water will spurt out and drip on the carpet and your head, and run down your arms. Gently spread the liquid on the surface. By the time you get to the end of the patch of wall you're working on, the initial application of solution has worked the dirt loose. Now go back to the starting point and again go over the area gently. No squeezing! This time, the dirt should be loosened by the chemicals in your cleaning solution and it will come off and soak into the sponge. In the other hand, folded to perfection, is your cleaning cloth, with which you quickly wipe and buff the area before it dries. No rinsing is necessary. The wiping will not only remove the remaining soap and dirt, but will polish off the scum that so often shows streaks on washed walls.

Now the critical procedure: Hold the sponge over the empty bucket and *squeeze,* don't wring (you only wring your hands or a chicken neck). When you squeeze the sponge, the dirty solution will go into the empty bucket, leaving the sponge damp and clean. Again dip the sponge ¼ inch into the bucket

3

Squeeze dirty sponge into empty bucket.

Dip into solution again & repeat.

of clean solution and repeat the process until the room is bright and clean.

You'll notice the empty bucket beginning to fill with filthy black gunk and the cleaning solution is still crystal clear. That's because when you dip the wrung-out damp sponge each time, the solution soaks into the squeezed hungry sponge, and the dirt never touches the solution. This means that every drop going on each new section of wall is powerful, unpolluted cleaning solution which is really doing most of the work. The old method you once used, scrubbing, dipping your sponge in the solution, wringing it, and scrubbing again, always left your cleaning water murky and filthy and thus without cleaning power. It would streak the walls and have to be changed every 15 minutes, taking up a lot of time and wasting a lot of cleaning solution. With the two-bucket method you don't spend time scrubbing, just applying and removing. And the towel dries and polishes walls three times as well as the old rags you once used.

2

Wipe sponged area with folded cleaning cloth.

When you finish, the empty bucket will be full of dirty water.

And your cleaning solution will still be crystal clear—the chemical was working for you!

Another advantage to this method of cleaning is that you won't have to cover everything because there will be little or no dripping. (If you have a grand piano which a drop might hurt, don't take the chance: Throw a light sheet of plastic over it.) Upholstered furniture can usually be moved out of the way rather than covered. A drop of ammonia solution won't hurt anything if it's removed immediately. If it's not it may spot or ruin the finish.

Besides doing a 70% faster and better job with this two-bucket technique, there are two more great "Life after Housework savers":

1. You will never dump and refill another bucket of solution. One healthy bucket of water and 13¢ worth of solution will do your whole house!

2. The dirty water . . . you will love it. In fact you will have a special relationship to it. Before, all your evidence of toil and accomplishment went down the drain; now you have it for show. I've seen women save it for days. (Bottle it and place it on the mantel.) I guarantee it will be the best, most heartwarming exhibit in your housekeeping "museum."

"Outside walls" (the inside surface of exterior walls) will be dirtier than inside or "partition" walls, so don't be surprised. If you can't see where you're going when you wash, forget it—it doesn't need washing! When you run into marks and spots on the walls that do not come clean when you wash them, just leave them until you finish. Then come back and try first to remove them by rubbing hard with a cleaning cloth and a little solution. Toothpaste, peanut butter, or abrasive cleansers will always get them, but they will also take off the paint or kill the sheen on the wall. Don't clean the spots before you wash the whole wall down—they might come off with the first washing. LET THE SOLUTION DO THE WORK! Most marks on walls can be removed by simply finding the same base cleaning agent. On a tar spot, for example, you can scrub and rub with high-powered cleaners, sweat and swear, and not get the spot; a little solvent-base turpentine or paint thinner will remove it in three seconds and not hurt the wall. Use your head, not your hands. With this method, you won't scour the paint off or streak the surfaces.

Go easy on the solution. You'll be shocked what too much will do for you!

Enameled Walls

When cleaning enamel-painted bathrooms, halls, or kitchen areas, use the same procedure, with one simple adjustment: Keep the drying towels cleaner and drier, because enamel needs more polishing and a drier surface than flat paint. Wipe marks will not show on flat paints, but they will show even on perfectly clean enamel. Those circular wipe marks that you can't see when you finish (but can later on in certain light) are caused by rags; rags can't/won't buff dry your walls. I was called back on many jobs during my first year of cleaning to remove streaks that weren't there when I left. Since that day 15 years ago when I began to use terry cleaning cloths I haven't been called back for a case of "enamel streak" on a single job.

Cleaning Woodwork

You can wash the woodwork or baseboards while doing the walls, but I seldom do. Because woodwork is covered with lint, hair, etc., that will get into your sponge and be difficult to get out. Wait until you are finished washing the room and you have a damp cloth remaining from the wall washing. Then wash the baseboard with it, cleaning it and picking up all the residue, then use your sponge and a fresh cleaning towel to finish it up, if need be, mark- and lint-free.

How to Clean Paneling

On paneling, use only a mild vegetable oil, soap (I like Lin-sol), or neutral cleaner, and apply it sparingly with a sponge. Then dry-buff it with a cleaning cloth, with the grain. If you dry it with the grain, occasional streaks will never be noticed. A clean, dry surface on a paneled wall is much better than covering the paneling with "El Gunko" panel polish and cleaners which leave a sticky surface to collect and hold handprints and every passing particle of dirt and dust. Remember that raw wood and other unfinished paneling must be coated with a finish so moisture won't penetrate the wood. Then you'll be cleaning on a finish, not the wood surface—it's faster, and much easier on the wood!

HOW TO CLEAN

Paneled walls. Use the same procedure as for painted walls. Use neutral cleaner with minimum moisture and buff dry with grain of wood.

Vinyl walls. Use the cleaner recommended by the manufacturer with minimum moisture. Use no corrosive material. Dry thoroughly.

Wallpaper. Use chemically treated dry sponge and clean with flow of design.

Cleaning Ceilings

Ceilings are always tough to clean even when they are easy (slick enamel, no texture or special finish of any kind). There is some good news and bad news for you ladies who for years have had aching arms and back and neck from working above your head. The bad news first: A physiologist told me that the muscle structure of a woman's torso is built to transfer the weight of a child carried while pregnant to the shoulders. Hence when a woman works above her head she is pulling *against* these muscles and finds it much more difficult than a man does. The good news is: what an excuse to get your husband to do the high work (such as ceilings)!

About 80% of your ceilings don't need washing (ceiling washing is tough even for experienced experts). Use a dry sponge, and if a few flyspecks remain, dip a Q-Tip in white shoe polish and mask them. If a ceiling, due to its texture, cigarette smoke stains, pole lamp scars, tough water leak stains (common in trailers), etc., poses a major cleaning chore, roll a coat of paint on. Ceilings are easier and faster areas to paint than to wash. If you try to wash (doing it Aslett style) and you get streaks or "lap-over" lines, don't walk your new redwood plank—it probably isn't your fault.

It is common for the builder to leave bare texture unpainted in a new home. When in five to seven years the ceiling needs cleaning, it can't be washed because the texture (which is sheet rock mud topping compound) will dissolve when water touches it. So one coat of latex paint should be rolled on, which "fills" the texture and leaves the ceiling fantastic. Five years later when you try to wash it (especially where the roller lines lap over), the moisture gets to the mud (which turns brown when wet), and you have a streak. So always paint two coats on an unpainted ceiling and it will be sealed enough to clean.

Take down the light fixtures first and pour cleaning solution on them and let them set while you clean the room. This keeps you from cutting your arms on them as you are cleaning the ceiling. After you finish the room, use a cleaning cloth to wipe the loosened film and dirt from the fixture. Rinse with hot water, dry, and put back up immediately.

Acoustical tile ceilings generally won't show dirt until it is too late to clean them. Clean annually with a dry sponge. If you fail to properly care for an acoustical tile ceiling, you'll have no choice but to paint it. That ruins the looks and the acoustics.

Washing closets: I'd wash the inside of the closets once every 20 years or so. They generally take longer than the whole room, and besides, nobody ever sees them anyway.

Don't Forget the Doors

There is an old business rule somebody installed as a proverb which in essence says, "20% of the workers do 80% of the work. 80% of our time is spent on 20% of our problems." It is called the Law of 80-20 and in one instance in the house holds true.

Our doors get 80% more use than any part of the house, yet we spend far less than 20% of our chore time keeping them clean and looking sharp. Doors are so taken for granted we seldom appreciate their contribution to a neat, attractive house. I once gave my wife a rest and got the house in top shape. When I finished my cleaning marathon, for some reason the house still looked unfinished. When I looked everything over, I found the floor glistening, the walls clean, no dust anywhere—but the *doors* had marks from hands, scratches from carrying groceries and suitcases through and knocking against them, the bottoms had black marks from kicks, mop and vacuum bumps, etc. Most of my doors are natural wood with clear finish. Some are painted. The painted doors were cleaned with a soft scrubbing sponge. If marks and nicks were present or the doors were dull, I simply repainted them. The natural wood I scrubbed with a good ammonia solution and a nylon pad. I cleaned with the grain of the wood and rinsed the door. It was now clean, but a little dull. I made sure it was dry and with some extra-fine sandpaper, I again went over the door, lightly, with the grain. The sanding removed lint, dust, and hair particles that got in the previous coat of finish. I took a cloth dampened with mineral spirits (paint thinner works, too) and wiped the door to get off every speck of lint and dust. By the way, I left the doors on while doing all this and put cardboard under them to protect the rug/floor. I applied a coat of low-gloss varnish—or a polyurethane finish—to each door (even on the tops), rolling it on so it was evenly distributed and then brushing with the grain. This prevents runs and misses. Let them dry. If you use the right material, it will dry in only three or four hours. You won't believe the difference it will make in your doors' appearance and the ease of keeping them clean! It will take just a few hours and will help preserve and protect the doors from future abuse.

Pick a day when the house is quiet—signs and warnings about keeping out of varnish aren't heeded. Do it on a dry summer day and the drying time will go fast. On a rainy day it can take 50% longer to dry. As soon as your bedroom door is dry enough to close, take a rest. You deserve it for all the time and money you have saved.

14

Painting Without Fainting

The construction company has just finished Betty Betterhouse's new home. Painting is all that is left to do before she can move in. The construction foreman put a beautiful texture on the living room ceiling, some gorgeous unfinished wood paneling downstairs, and some fine decorative masonry block work in the basement game room. Not wanting to cover these natural surfaces, which were indeed beautiful, Betty asks that the painters not touch the living room ceiling. She has them leave the wood paneling natural, and two light coats of paint are applied to the masonry wall in the basement game room.

Betty moves in, and for two years she enjoys the new home, and she enjoys keeping it neat and clean. Gradually, she becomes frustrated with three areas in her house: the living room ceiling, the wood paneling, and the masonry wall. Some flyspecks, a fizzing soft drink, and moving a pole lamp have left their marks on the pretty white textured ceiling. When Betty mixes some cleaning solution and tries to remove the blemishes, she is horrified at the results: When the liquid hits the ceiling, the texture dissolves and comes off. Although the texture had seemed to be as hard as concrete or plaster, it wasn't. The texture was composed of perfa-tape compound which, although it hardens, will soften again when it is wet. Betty touches up the marks with a little white shoe polish, but eventually she has only one alternative and that is to paint the ceiling.

One coat of an off-white latex paint covers the ceiling and it looks great, but its cleanability is still doubtful. One coat of paint is enough to prevent the texture from *dissolving* when it is washed, but streaks or lines will probably occur because some moisture will penetrate the paint and react with the texture. Betty really should give the ceiling two or more coats of paint in order for it to be cleanable in the future.

Betty greatly enjoys her natural wood because of its homeyness and warm appearance. One afternoon, Betty's children get into the Crisco and the crayons, and a generous percentage of the mess that's distributed throughout the house ends up on the wood wall. It penetrates into the wood, and no matter how she scrubs or what formula she tries, the spots and marks remain visible.

Betty should have painted the wood with a low-luster "velvet clear finish." This would have penetrated the wood and formed a membrane or protective shield. The shield would keep grease stains and other foreign marks from soaking into the wood's surface. A flat or satin finish varnish will dry with a low shine and the natural look of wood is preserved.

The masonry cinderblock walls in the basement receive their share of the recreation room residue and need to be cleaned. When Betty tries to wash the painted blocks, she finds it almost impossible to get the dirt out of the pits and joints common in masonry construction. Betty should stop washing and apply another two coats of heavy enamel paint. This extra paint will fill the remaining rough spots in the wall and will make a good washable surface for the future.

The partnership of painting and cleaning can be an important housecleaning ally. I was a licensed paint contractor for several years and am convinced that a little painting wisdom can save you a considerable amount of cleaning woes and hundreds of hours of cleaning time. Books of "slick quick" painting tips have been peddled for years, but haven't convinced many homemakers that the task of redecorating a home, inside or out, is easy and fun. Painting is generally considered a dreaded necessity! Painting can, however, be a rewarding physical and emotional experience for you if you make it easy.

Almost anyone can be a good painter. The basic cause of the despair and discouragement suffered by the home painter is that by the time you get fairly proficient in the task, it ends. It is three or four years before you pick up the paint tools and start the learning process all over again. If you would keep it up for a few weeks longer, you would conquer most of the problem areas and enjoy it. Don't fall for gimmicks, miracle tools, or "do-it-yourself paint." Brushes, rollers, and spray guns can do it all, and in the long run, they are easier once you learn how to use them.

Summing up all painting wisdom in one volume is unimaginable, and doing it in one chapter of a housecleaning book is not possible, so I resort to some brief instructions.

Prepare Before You Paint

"Efficient" painting begins before you paint; preparing yourself, your furnishings, and the painting surface. The following suggestions will benefit all three of you. The mental anguish of mess and smell is what most people dread in painting. Minimize it!

1.   *Clean.* If walls are very greasy or dirty, you should clean them prior to painting, using a good strong solution that will quickly remove the dirt (don't worry about hurting the surface). Here is a place where 70% of the time the dry sponge is a lifesaver. You can dry-sponge a bedroom down in minutes, then

paint it. For other surfaces and problems, ask at your paint store—such service is part of the paint price. A rented pressure washer can have the exterior of a dirty house ready to go in hours.

2. *Prepare.* Use prepared spackle mix to patch holes. Let it dry. After sanding it, coat it with shellac to seal it. This will prevent dull spots in your paint job. As for nicks, bare wood, etc., always follow directions on the paint can. Use primer and *then* paint when surfaces require preconditioning—don't just use two coats of paint! A coat of primer undercoating is much better than a coat of paint as an undercoat.

3. *Protect.* Tromping through sheets of newspaper, half of them stuck to your feet with paint drops, while trying to untangle flimsy plastic dropcloths for your furniture will remove any doubts in your mind as to why Hitler was a painter and wallpaperer. Use old sheets to cover your furnishings and canvas dropcloths for floors. They're not expensive, will last for years, and you will find many other uses for them.

4. *Ventilate.* For some reason most people think that heat is what's needed to dry things. Wrong. It's air circulation that does most of the drying. Even cool air circulating freely will dry paint faster than a sealed house with the heat up to 80°. Breathing paint fumes reduces your physical efficiency and produces mental discouragement. Get plenty of air flow—it helps you and the paint!

Use the right paint. By using a top-grade washable paint, you can paint less. Handprints, flyspecks, food or splashes, hair oil, etc., penetrate into flat paint and generally cannot be removed. Use enamel paint for more efficient cleaning. Buy well-known, high-quality brands. The extra $5 spent on a gallon of paint is one of the best cleaning investments you will ever make.

Select a "reasonable" color. Use as much of the same color throughout your home as possible. Too many homes look like a circus wagon because homemakers are still trying to "decorate" their homes with paint. The color and style of modern furniture, drapes, and carpet do a fine job of giving a home richness and taste. Using a soft off-white shade on all the walls, ceilings, and woodwork will allow your furnishings to flatter your home and will simplify your painting because it won't go out of style. (And all your touch-up paint is in one can.)

Choosing the room color from a color chip has caused many a nervous collapse after the paint is on. Paint is always darker and brighter than you expected or wanted. When you get the shade and color you think you want, move about two shades lighter on the color chart. You'll probably be much happier with the results.

Buy professional equipment and take care of it. A deeper roller pan or bucket with screen will boost efficiency and lessen the possibility of spills. Good brushes and a heavy-duty roller will also cover better, apply faster and more evenly.   Learn to use roller extension handles. They work beautifully with professional tools and a two-foot effort with your arms will project a six-foot effort on the painting surface. Again, they will be awkward at first, but they are faster than holding a roller frame in your hand. (They also get you back from your work so you can see what you are doing.)

Use your stepladder, regular ladder, or plank and box. They will make your painting task a lot easier.

Some Tips on Technique

● Prevent drips. When you first open the paint bucket, use a screwdriver or nail and punch several holes inside the lid groove. All the excess paint that used to run down the side will run back into the bucket and when the lid goes on, it will seal tight without squirting paint all over the side or all over you.

● "Thinning" doesn't hurt paint. Getting paint to a flowing consistency will create a brushed or rolled surface as smooth as silk. Use a recommended thinner and spirits (not gasoline or other substitutes). Letting paint run off a dipped paint stir stick is a good way to judge consistency. If enamel runs to a point two inches below the stick, it is just right. Solvent evaporation causes many enamel paints to get "heavy" when stored or while in use. Thin it down! Some paint will appear too thin already. Insufficient stirring is the most probable cause of thin paint—the heavy pigments are likely to have settled on the bottom. Always have the paint store shake the can on their machine. It is much easier and safer—the lid could come off while you are shaking it. There is a tendency to not stir varnish enough. Because it is clear, it looks mixed and fools the user. Varnish driers settle out in the bottom, and if not stirred well, varnish will take forever to dry!

● Most people paint too much. When you paint too much, the sharp, crisp, trim edges and corners become so gobbed they make the house look cheap and sloppy. Any chips in the surface, which happen in even the best-kept homes, are deep and ugly and almost impossible to blend in when the base is over-painted.

● Always drag the last stroke of the brush *into* the finished area. Don't pull it away. If you brush into the finished area, there won't be a brush mark.

● Even though you have rolled over a surface once and it appears covered, it isn't.

Cross over it more than once. The first roller pass appears adequate, but small "pinholes" or air holes are there that will not show until the paint is dry.

Cleanup

The most dreaded part of painting won't be a chore at all if you always scrape the paint out of the roller before you try to wash or clean it out. Use a paint stick or putty knife to do this messy job. Some rollers can hold about a cup of paint, and leaving it in results in a waste of paint, solvent, and cleaning time. If you don't scrape it, you can wash it with soap, squeeze it, and never seem to get anywhere—paint will come out of rollers forever. If you've scraped it properly, you can clean a roller in minutes with a small amount of thinner. Once the roller is scraped dry, place it in a pan of thinner to loosen the remaining paint. Don't waste your time squeezing and massaging with your hands. Just spin the roller vigorously on a pole, post (or your arm, if you're desperate). Centrifugal force will throw the moisture effectively out of the nap. If any of it gets on you, it wipes off easier than laboring on a roller for 10 minutes in a pan full of thinner.

Get all the paint out of the brush and dip it in the brush cleaner or solvent and swish it around to release (dissolve) the paint on the bristles. Again, a quick spin between your palms will accomplish more than 10 minutes of sloshing. A little vegetable oil on the brush will preserve and soften it for future use. When finished, seal the brush in aluminum foil.

Always keep leftover paint for touch-up. Seal it well, and label it accordingly. Small baby food bottles make excellent touch-up containers.

Wallpaper Removal

In the first 15 years of my cleaning contracting, I did an enormous amount of wallpaper removing. You might like to know in a few sentences what it took me 15 years to learn.

If you can avoid removing wallpaper, make every effort to do so. But if you can't, then I would recommend the following: First, you'll waste your time and money getting steamers, magic wallpaper dissolvers, boards with nails in them, and other gimmickry. I stewed and sweated with all of them for hours, thinking something must be wrong with me, because the steamers were worn out by previous users. (Little did I know that all of them had had the same results and the same paranoid feeling about their efforts.) With all of their "magic," and five helpers, the lady of the house and I would end up with putty chisels or knives, picking, gouging, and scraping off scraps of wallpaper.

The best thing to do is to get a bucket of warm water, a big sponge, and a scaffold. Set up your plank so that you can get at the entire surface you want removed. Then wet one end of the area down as heavily as possible (just so it doesn't run down the wall too much). Cover the entire area, then go back and start over again, again, and again. It really isn't much work, and is rather boring, but keep wetting it. After about 30 minutes of wetting, check a place or two. If it is quite loose, pull the paper off; if not, keep wetting. Don't get anxious. If you wet it enough, the stuff will come off in a big sheet. Then wipe the soggy glue off the wall so it will be in good shape. If wallpaper has 10 coats of paint over it . . . panel the wall or move!

15

Shorter Visits to the Bathroom

The restroom in the commercial building was a sight to behold. A line of sinks stretched to infinity, and the toilet stalls looked like the Santa Anita starting gate. This huge restroom was used by 250 people, and it just radiated cleanliness. The chrome glistened, and the white porcelain of the sinks and toilets sparkled germ-free. All toilet paper and hand-towel dispensers were filled. And the matron only spent an hour per day to keep it that way.

Clean Your Bathroom in 3½ Minutes

Considering the average home's size and use, and that matron's production time, you should be able to keep your bathroom in

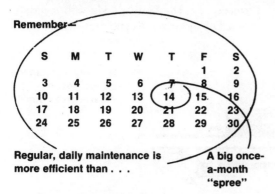

Remember—

S	M	T	W	T	F	S
					1	2
3	4	5	6	7	8	9
10	11	12	13	14	15	16
17	18	19	20	21	22	23
24	25	26	27	28	29	30

Regular, daily maintenance is more efficient than . . .

A big once-a-month "spree"

that same immaculate condition in 3½ minutes per day! Sound impossible? Not if you follow some professional techniques. The "commercial approach" to cleaning your bathroom is simple and will save you time, the secret, of course, being to keep it clean a few minutes a day rather than in a big once-a-week clean-and-scrub siege. The preventive cleaning approach here is smart.

Tools and supplies again are an important factor. You'll have to bite your lip and disregard most of the old standbys like abrasive cleansers, acid bowl cleaners, deodorant sprays, magic toilet spices, perfumed blocks, and blue bowl seltzers. If you maintain your bathroom regularly and efficiently, you'll seldom need to use any of these.

Essential Supplies

For annual removal of hard-water or mineral buildup, the old cleanser or mild phosphoric acid has its use, even by the professional. The best procedure to follow, however, is a regular cleaning program that eliminates the need for abrasive cleansers and acids.

To avoid wasted time, damage to fixtures, and poor-quality results, you should go

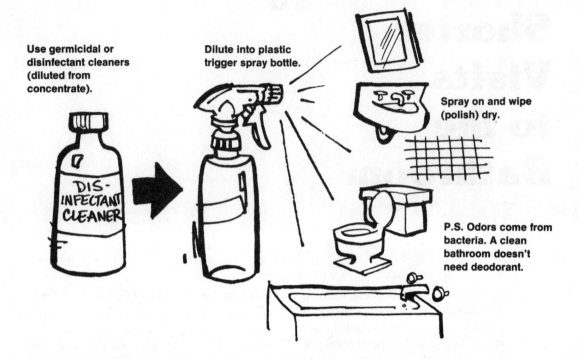

Use germicidal or disinfectant cleaners (diluted from concentrate).

Dilute into plastic trigger spray bottle.

Spray on and wipe (polish) dry.

P.S. Odors come from bacteria. A clean bathroom doesn't need deodorant.

DIS-INFECTANT CLEANER

to the local janitorial supply house and purchase scented or unscented *disinfectant cleaner concentrate* (it's what hospitals use). This liquid, if diluted according to the directions on the bottle and used correctly, will clean quickly and efficiently, and eradicate or retard bacterial growth. This will eliminate smells and the need for the expensive perfumed preparations you have been using. While at the janitorial supply house, pick up one plastic spray bottle for each bathroom so the bottle can be left in the room.

Once the spray bottle is filled with the water and disinfectant cleaner in the correct proportion, the only other tools you need are a *cleaning cloth or towel* and a *white two-sided scouring sponge* of cellulose and nylon mesh (for dislodging any persistent residue). Spray and wipe the mirror if it's spotted. It not, leave it alone. Next, spray the hardware, sink, countertops (spray ahead so the cleaner will soften and break down soil); wipe and buff the surfaces dry. They will sparkle with a glossy sheen. Do shower stalls and tubs next. Do the

Harsh, abrasive scouring pads will gradually eat off chrome and porcelain and pit surfaces.

Ouch!!

green

white

Use a white scrubbing sponge, not an abrasive green one.

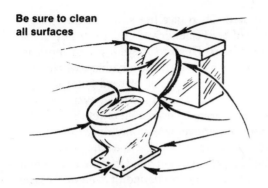

Be sure to clean all surfaces

toilet stool last, and be sure to get the base of it. The reason for doing this last is to avoid transporting the worst germ concentration to the faucet handles. Once the upper fixtures are clean, fall to your knees (one minute won't hurt you). Spray the floor, and with the already damp terry towel, wipe it up. This method is 10 minutes faster and better than mixing up disinfectant mop water and fumbling around with a mop in a 20-square-foot area.

The Benefits of Preventive Maintenance

It takes only minutes to clean a bathroom the spray-disinfectant way, and if a spray bottle and cloth are left in the room, you can get your bathroom spotless while you are waiting for Junior to go potty or for the sink to fill up. The system works only if you clean the

THIS WILL KEEP BUILDUP DOWN:

If hard-water rings and deposits get ahead of you, use chemicals occasionally.

Application of a mild phosphoric solution will dissolve hard-water scale and soap scum.

bathroom regularly, however. This keeps hard-water deposits, soap scum, toilet bowl lines, and other soils from building up and cementing on. The basic reason you needed abrasive cleansers and acids (and dynamite) to clean the bathroom in the past was that buildup accumulated to the point of no return and had to be ground off instead of wiped off.

Minimize the use of:

Observing the many hundreds of houses I've cleaned in my career, more than 50% of the bathrooms (tubs, sinks, plastic tub and shower units, etc.) have had damage from improper use of acids, cleansers, and abrasive pads. This is a great reason to use the disinfectant cleaner/spray bottle system from the start. Your chrome, plastic, fiberglass, marble, etc., will remain bright and sound. If you have damaged fixtures, you will have some difficulty using anything because porous surfaces collect gunk fast and clean slow. Many of these surfaces—especially the shower area—will benefit from a coat of paste wax, which helps repel the gunk and hard-water buildup. After attending my seminar, many a housekeeper minimizes the problem of shower buildup by simply hanging a 10- or 12-inch squeegee in the shower. It takes only 15 seconds for the user to leave the wall dry and clean after a shower. (Besides, squeegeeing in the nude is a unique experience!)

Be careful what you soak in tubs and sinks overnight. Extended exposure to some normally harmless cleaners will often pit the surface.

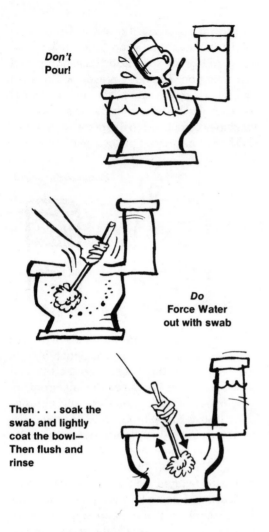

Don't Pour!

Do Force Water out with swab

Then . . . soak the swab and lightly coat the bowl— Then flush and rinse

Cleaning Toilets

Briskly scrubbing inside a toilet bowl with a bowl brush daily for a few seconds will retard buildup and remove discoloration and lines. If you need to remove old buildup in the toilet, do it right. Do not pour steaming acid into the water-filled bowl and slosh it around. Dilution with water neutralizes the power of any bowl cleaner. Instead, grasp a swab (see equipment chart, Chapter 2) and push it quickly up and down in the bowl toward the bottom. All the water will "vanish" and leave a "bare bowl" (no free advertising or pun in-

tended). Then give the swab a light application of bowl cleaner and coat the inside of the toilet bowl. Flush to rinse. If a ring remains, don't get excited and acid-bath the whole unit. The ring is the result of hard-water deposit that's left as water in the toilet evaporates. A pumice stone or even a little wet-dry sandpaper will remove almost any ring. Remember to brush the bowl once in a while to prevent buildup. And bear in mind that bleach is not a good cleaning compound. It is an aggressive oxidizing agent. It appears to clean things, but this appearance is often deceptive. The oxidizing or whitening of stains, toilet rings, rust stains, etc., generally doesn't remove them, but only bleaches or camouflages them. Bleach will eventually break down chrome and Formica and other plastic laminates. Keep it out of your bathrooms!

Toilet-tank capsules that turn the water blue don't do much for maintaining toilets, since many of them are only colored bleaching agents. Their greatest value is psychological. If you practice good cleaning habits in the bathroom, you won't need them.

Caution . . . .

Bathroom acids can splash!

How to Get Rid of Mildew

When warm, humid weather and spores of mold team up, mildew can grow on everything, including drawers, closets, books, and shoes. For the first 20 years of my life, I thought mildew was something that appeared on roses and alfalfa. Since entering the cleaning business, I've been bombarded with the mildew question: "How do we get rid of it?" The best way to get rid of it is to prevent it. (Another inducement to follow the advice in Chapter 4—who wants 70% mildewed junk?) Keeping kitchen grease, soil, and other foreign substances cleaned up removes the growth bed for mildew. Using disinfectant in the bathroom and shower areas discourages its growth there. Keep the house clean, well-ventilated, and as dry as possible. Use silica gel or calcium chloride granules if necessary to retard mildew. Bleach "kills" mildew, but won't prevent it from returning.

Doorknobs and Handbags

One of the most unsanitary items in the home is the doorknob. It wouldn't hurt, while armed with a spray bottle of disinfectant cleaner, to go through the house and spray and wipe all the doorknobs occasionally. Another unsanitary carry-over from restrooms that all women should be aware of is the purse or handbag. Purses are often placed on dining tables (right where your salad fork is) after having been set on the floor alongside the toilet in a public restroom. Avoid this unappetizing practice! Set your purse by your chair—and use the purse shelves provided in public restrooms, when available.

16

Designing Your Own Efficiency

I am a firm believer in personal inspiration and revelation, and I am furthermore convinced that women are brighter, and more ingenious, than men. Most of the time *you* can figure things out better and quicker than "Dr. Home Advice" can in his column or book. When you meet a problem that is unique to you, nothing is more rewarding than using your own ability to zero in on it and solve it. You say you hate to paint the inside of the cupboards? Pick up your big furry cat and the neighbor's shaggy dog, dip them in the roller pan of paint, throw them both inside the cupboard, close the door, and if a fight doesn't immediately ensue, beat a little war rhythm on the side of the cupboard with your fists. The stimulated animals will evenly and expertly distribute the paint on the inside surface, and all you'll have to do is touch up a few tracks and give the animals a mineral spirits bath.

This may be a far-fetched example, but what I'm trying to say is that nothing is impossible. Don't think negatively—and don't restrict your thinking when you're trying to solve a problem. Your personal ingenuity is limitless! Everyone reading this book has had from 1 to 100 ideas that she was going to build into her dream home to save housework. Most of these ideas were brilliant in concept, workable, economical, practical, and capable of saving millions of hours of household toil. It is sad, however, that coming from the best source in the world, the homemaker, not even a minute percentage of these ideas have been developed. The excitement of that special timesaving idea was lost in the hassle of satisfying financial, federal, FHA, and other rules. Thus people end up taking what they can get—a plain old house crowded with things that require maintenance time the rest of their lives. Most homeowners are still hop-

109

ing that some brilliant, resourceful, pioneering young architect will major in designing "chore-free homes" and liberate us all with one grand swoop of the drafting pen. Well, so far it hasn't happened, and you can rest assured that it won't happen . . . at least not in that way. The *homemaker* is the source of power in such a revolution. Will she respond? I hope so.

Again it all boils down to how valuable your time is. Work can be lessened, and time saved, by good maintenance planning and decorating. For example, bathrooms bedecked with velvet toilet covers, deep-pile carpets, and a couple of your favorite oil paintings will be a drain to maintain unless you have limitless hours to clean or have an outhouse fixation of some kind. A bathroom is no place for elaborate bookcases, statues, or other unmaintainable furniture and fixtures. Keep in mind the following:

1. Will it clean?

2. Will it last?

3. Is it usable?

If you weigh these items carefully, it might save you a lot of hours cleaning hand-carved toilet seats!

Designing work out of your home is unquestionably the best approach to household freedom. Everyone living in a house or desiring to build a new one, or buy an old one, can invent, manufacture, and install in her home anything she wants. If your time is constantly used up running outside your rambling ranch house trying to locate or keep an eye on your children, go to an army surplus store and pick up a used submarine periscope and mount it in your kitchen instead of running in and out all the time. Just say, "Up scope," and scan the yard, never leaving the house. (Ridiculous? Not so, if it works—and suits *your* needs.)

Be bold enough to think up and design your own laborsaving plans and devices.

If you hate to move and dust furniture and want to have groups of people in your home on special occasions, dig a pit for a sunken front room and build in stationary padded furniture. I told you earlier how we did it: It sat up to 40 and there wasn't a stick of furniture to clean. If you've got husky boys who are going to fight and wrestle, build their dresser into a stagecoach between two built-to-the-floor beds. Carpet the top of the dresser so they can play cowboys and roll down onto the bed. It will save a torn-up room and cleanup time, and besides, it'll be great sport for the boys. When they grow up and begin to act like humans, get them human beds! If you don't like to wash and paint walls, carpet them—they'll be a cinch to maintain.

If you are a short or tall family, hang your closet rods, toilet paper dispensers, doorknobs, and mirrors where you don't have to tiptoe or stoop to navigate through the house. If you run your home like a garage, then put a drain in the center of the floor.

Some Time Robbers to Avoid

● *Indented or embossed tile or linoleum.* It looks great, but recessed surfaces collect dirt, are hard to sweep, and will gradually fill with wax.

- *Indoor-outdoor carpet.* It shows everything. It's difficult to clean and adds zero plushness to a home.

- *Highly textured walls and ceilings.* They hold dirt and are a spider's paradise. They're hard to clean and paint.

- *Unfinished wood.* Looks nice and rustic, but once it's soiled, you've had it. Wood should always be sealed and finished.

- *Fancy engraved hardware.* This takes time to keep up and provides breeding grounds for bugs.

- *Extremely high ceilings.* Although it is impressive and prestigious to have a couple of 25- to 30-foot ceilings in your house, they are hard to maintain and energy-wasteful.

- *Multi-surface furniture and fixtures.* Every surface needs maintenance—the less the better. A louvered door, for example, has much more surface than a simple, smooth door.

- *Dark colors* (furniture, floors, counter tops) require more daily upkeep than medium-colored items (dark colors show dust and spots—*everything!*).

- *Decoration clusters.* One big nice picture sure beats a dusty clump of 40 little ones (and cheats spiders out of bases).

- *Free-standing appliances*—(washers, dryers, ovens, stoves, refrigerators, dishwashers). They have *five* sides to keep clean (most built-ins have one or two).

- *Carpet in high-risk areas.* It takes ten minutes to clean up your jam sandwich from a carpeted kitchen floor, but only ten seconds off a hard-surface floor.

- Avoid windows in areas where you don't really need them. A window, because it's a light source, draws everything from flies to kids to animals to moisture. And windows require drapes, shades, and curtains. Window areas are high maintenance areas—you'll spend much more time cleaning a windowed area than you will on an equivalent stretch of wall.

You could continue this list for hours. Do so before you build or take over another house. Once you arrive at a timesaving idea and are sure that you want it, *do* it, not bullying your way, but checking and working it out with the builder, engineer, architect, or whomever is in charge. Remember, most people are chickenhearted when it comes to departing from the beaten track, and that includes many professional people. On the other hand, a little timely professional advice may keep you out of trouble. For example, I designed all of the lights in our home to be wall-mounted 6½ feet from the floor. The purpose was to eliminate ladders and reduce physical damage to the house and safety risks in light bulb changing. It was a great plan. I picked out some handsome, expensive, frosted hexagon fixtures and mounted them. We couldn't see a thing! Wall lights, especially the frosted ones, are not designed to shed light. I now have 90 individual light fixtures in my home and still can't see much without a candle or a miner's hat. A few minutes of professional advice would have showed me how to save 40 of those light fixtures (and some expensive energy payments) and still get adequate light.

Good design means wise selection of paint, wall coverings, and carpets. Design, fix up, or rebuild according to your lifestyle, and you won't regret it! Here is a "test" list you might review for your house. You can come up with the details to fit your taste and energy level if you'll apply these maintenance-minded criteria:

Ease of maintenance. Once a surface is subjected to use, it will become soiled, worn, and dusty. A surface should be *eco-*

nomically cleanable (from both a time and money standpoint).

Accessibility. All surfaces, appliances, and decorations must be located for easy access. "Under, up, over, or in back of" must be eliminated.

Replaceability. Ruined or worn areas or items someday have to be replaced. Choosing standard sizes and styles will make this a lot easier.

Durability. Materials or structures must be able to resist wear from natural or human abuse.

Serviceability. Is manpower or equipment conveniently available to clean or repair the item?

Safety. Is it safe?

What About Being a Professional Housecleaner?

17

Can you picture yourself next Monday morning? It's 9:00. All of your housework is done. Your home is organized, and you are leaving it to go clean four other homes . . . for $10 an hour? No, it isn't a fantasy or a joke.

One of the biggest economic and social realities of the '80s is the two-career family. The effects of an extra job on family and marriage relationships can be problematical. But that doesn't eliminate many families' growing need for a second income. Homemakers with

12 children or no children have flocked to the job market in an attempt to meet ever-mounting inflation. In order to secure employment, most have found it necessary to purchase extra transportation, accept close to minimum-wage jobs, hire expensive child care services, and spend a lot of money on a business wardrobe. Actual benefits from most homemakers' second jobs would be questionable if both direct and indirect costs were calculated properly. Why go through the expense of all that overhead to gain a tiny per-

cent of income when you can double your profit for half the emotional and physical price you are paying? Why not start your own professional housecleaning business? It is not only possible, but will offer you some great personal and family advantages:

1. Excellent income: $10 to $20 per hour for your time.

2. Tax deductions and depreciation breaks.

3. The potential for family involvement.

4. The ability to work on your own schedule.

5. Rewarding social and educational experiences.

6. Regular physical exercise.

7. Equipment to do all your own housecleaning.

8. Opportunity to pick your own working associates.

Why get a job where you don't have time with your husband, or friends? Why have children you can't enjoy? Why fight traffic and parking and rigid schedules every day? Why answer to "bosses"? Why tolerate excessive deductions from your check? Why realize only a small amount of "clear" money for 40 hours of hard work? On your own terms and at your own energy level, in your own selected environment, you could make the same money in half the hours and feel better physically and emotionally.

The market for housework is wide open. There isn't a household in American that doesn't need housework done. The majority of struggling homemakers can't cope with their own housework, so that leaves the majority of your neighborhood or town needing help. You can provide it! Good professional housecleaning companies are almost nonexistent. Being a woman, you have a number of advantages over a male to land a professional housecleaning job. Homemakers are extremely particular as to who they turn loose in their house to clean, and you, another homemaker, will more easily win their trust. You'll love it, and it won't tax your own personal family life like a full-time job would. The predominant fear most people have about trying their own business is, "Can I get customers?" This will never be a problem if you do good quality work for an honest price. Even when I first started out, my success rate in getting the jobs that I bid was 9 out of 10. Here are a few strategies which will help you.

Learn to Bid Your Work

The first step is to learn to bid work! Don't work by the hour! Everybody in the world thinks a "cleaning lady" should get a few bucks an hour. If you quoted $5 an hour to wash someone's windows she would gasp unbelievingly at your nerve, even if you told her it would only take three hours ($15). However, if you said, as you wrote the price on your card and handed it to the homemaker, "I have looked at your windows carefully and feel for labor, materials, and equipment, I can do them for $30," she would nod gratefully. A set price is more acceptable than a per-hour rate for most homemakers.

The most asked question in the industry is "How do I know how much to bid?" That's easy. Figure how long it will take you and multiply by what you want to make an hour. The better and faster you become, the more you have to charge. After a few months, you'll know your actual production time and will be able to estimate closely. You'll over- or underestimate a few times (you might have to work free for a while)—and you'll learn from it. But once you get good, your confidence will "wax" strong, and you'll get almost every job you bid. This little table of costs will give you some guidance in getting started.

114

Bid Estimate Guide

Walls and ceilings	per sq. ft.	small room	medium room	large room
Cleaning				
Hall	3¢	$ 7	$10	$12
Den	3¢	11	16	20
Recreation room	3¢	18	25	30
Living room	3-4¢	18	26	36
Dining room	3-4¢	12	16	18
Bedroom	3-4¢	10	15	21
Entrance	4¢	5	8	13
Bathroom	4¢	5	8	12
Kitchen	4-5¢	14	25	35
Stair landing	5¢	12	14	20
Utility room	5¢	10	12	14

Hard-surface floors	lightly soiled	average	filthy
Clean	1¢ (per sq. ft.)	2¢ (per sq. ft.)	3¢ (per sq. ft.)
Clean and wax	3¢ ”	5¢ ”	7¢ ”
Strip and wax	8¢ ”	10¢ ”	12¢ ”
Carpets			
Vacuum and spot-clean	1¢ ”	2¢ ”	3¢ ”
Spin-surface	3¢ ”	4¢ ”	8¢ ”
Shampoo (extract)	8¢ ”	10¢ ”	12¢ ”
Windows (both sides)	3¢ ”	3¢ ”	4¢ ”
Small, accessible	3¢ ”	3¢ ”	4¢ ”
Large, accessible	2¢ ”	2¢ ”	3¢ ”
Small, inaccessible	4¢ ”	4¢ ”	5¢ ”
Large, inaccessible	2.5¢ ”	3¢ ”	4¢ ”

Upholstery	lightly soiled	average	filthy
Small chair	$2 (per item)	$3 (per item)	$5 (per item)
Large chair	5 ”	7 ”	8 ”
Small couch	8 ”	10 ”	14 ”
Large couch	12 ”	15 ”	22 ”
Furniture			
Clean and polish			
Small end table	1 ”	1.50 ”	2 ”
Average TV	2 ”	2.50 ”	3 ”
Piano	4 ”	4.75 ”	5.25 ”
Desks, dressers	3.50 ”	4 ”	5 ”

Commercial Janitorial	small office	medium office	large office
Square feet bid	5-8¢ sq. ft./ per month	5-6¢ sq. ft./ per month	4-5¢ sq. ft./ per month
Total cleaning production per hour	**light office** 3000 sq. ft.	**medium office** 2800 sq. ft.	**heavy office** 2000 sq. ft.

(total square footage quotes are of area actually cleaned or serviced)

Other business operation costs:
  Vehicle—charge 25¢ a mile
  Overhead—add 5% to your total bid to cover phone, advertising, etc.
  Maid work per hour if requested—$6-$6.50 contract amount.

(guide continues to next page)

If someone wants to rent or borrow your equipment and supplies—don't do it. You'll lose at every turn. Instead, encourage them to buy or make their own. Very few people know how to take care of professional equipment and damaged or lost parts or attachments can cost you a month's profit.

Be extremely careful about bidding or giving prices over the phone, or in conversation. There can be a big difference in two bedrooms exactly the same size and the same age of home. Type of paint, condition, location, accessibility, the personalities of people you will be working for, and many other factors can create a bidding problem if you don't look over a job in person.

Remember, this table is only a guide. You'll be able to plug your own figures in after a little experience. Who you work for as well as the quality of homes and furnishings you are working on will make a lot of difference in the amount of cleaning time required. Much depends on the area, size of rooms, types of paint on the wall (enamel or latex), who furnishes the equipment, who gets the area ready, how far you have to travel, etc. You will have a few losses, but that will stimulate your desire to be more accurate and you'll get good!

Always bid work. This is the basic formula of success in your own business. If it's bid and you work twice as hard, you can earn twice as much money by the hour.

Regular everyday housework type services (sweeping, vacuuming, dusting, etc.) are always in demand. But almost anyone can do that kind of housework, at about the same rate of production and speed, and this holds the cost or worth of such jobs down. Try to specialize in the areas where the homemaker struggles: floors, walls, window washing, rugs, etc. Competence in these areas will lead you to other, and even more lucrative jobs.

Unless the customer demands it, or unless the job is very small, never give a bid price at the time you go to look at a job. Leave the customer convinced that you are the best-qualified person to do the job and that she will be missing out if she doesn't have you do the work. (Brag on yourself.) Return home, prepare the bid, and mail it to the customer. Handing the customer a bid and standing and waiting for a decision creates an unpleasant atmosphere. Especially with large expenditures at stake, the customer likes to study the bid and think it over before making a commitment. A commitment given in haste or under pressure often develops into a bad customer relationship and often affects the job and the promptness with which the bill will be paid.

The proper conversation while the job is being estimated can make a big difference. If you can see that money is a problem at the moment, and if you know that her credit is good, let a prospective customer know that you are agreeable to arranging suitable terms. (Compensate for this in the bid.) Remember, some jobs you may consider small or common are great and expensive decisions for some customers. Take your time, examine the whole job, and add your personal touch to the negotiation. An unconcerned square-footage estimator divorces herself from this personal touch, which is one of the biggest factors in whether or not you get the job.

Helpful Techniques in Preparing a Bid

When preparing a bid, itemize and describe clearly the service you are going to provide. Picture words and specifics are much more effective than just stating the minimum of information. For example, here are two ways a job could be described in a bid to paint a floor:

Example A. Painting porch floor, one coat
gray enamel . $45.00

Example B. Preparation of complete rear porch floor area including light sanding, renailing protruding nails, removing all dust and foreign material, and applying one coat of Benjamin Moore Floor and Deck Enamel in Dover Gray color. Total cost. $44.50

Almost anyone would accept the second bid rather than the first one because it appears that she is getting more for her money. "Preparation" is simply getting the area ready, and both bids include that. But example B *tells* the customer about it. "Light sanding" means removing paint blisters or scaly areas, and "re-nailing protruding nails" may take three or four minutes. "Removing all dust and foreign material" just means sweeping the floor. Example A didn't even bother to tell the customer that the floor would be swept. "Applying" is a professional word; "painting" is Tom Sawyer stuff. When listed on a bid, professional-sounding words help sell the job.

For large or long-term jobs, your bid should be submitted with a one-page standard contract agreement form (such as the one shown on page 121). Most office supply stores have them; your name can be stamped or printed on the blank form. Once a relationship of trust is established, a contract may not be necessary on every job.

Getting Started

If you just follow the directions in this book, you'll know more about housecleaning than anyone you will ever work for. Every job will multiply your experience. You'll find with your skills you can consistently average $8 to $12 per hour. Sometimes you'll get as high as $25 per hour on special jobs.

The idea of getting started seems to cause even the most talented to shake in their boots. I know you can do it, and once you

start, you'll look back, after the first three jobs, and laugh at yourself for being nervous about trying it. Visions of arming yourself with a mop bucket and dustcloth and parading up and down the streets beating on doors for business are out. You want to go to work, not jail! Here is a starting place.

1. **Get a name and a slogan.** Just think—a chance to name your own company! Avoid personal names like Mabel's Cleaning, Betty's Broom Service, Jones Cleaners. Instead, use names like Century, Belair (like car names) except relate it to homes. Such names have a ring of authority, and will inspire greater confidence. (Would you rather eat at Myrtle's Cafe or The Sea Galley?)

House Cleaning / Janitorial Service / Painting / Rug & Upholstery

2. **Have cards or leaflets printed.** Always use a picture or visual symbol on your "advertising" literature of any kind. A bit of creativity, some rub-on lettering, and a little free help from the printer will give you an inexpensive but effective tool to attract business. Avoid tacky "clip art" decorations. Be fresh and original.

Print 200-500 or more for the best cost breaks. Use a local press.

3. **Check into the rules and regulations.** Make a call to state, federal, and local tax offices and the telephone company and explain to them the scale on which you intend

to operate. If you're just going to do an occasional job, with no employees, they will probably say "no problem." But if you are going to operate on a large scale and hire a couple of neighbors and have a vehicle, etc., it's best to inform the agencies involved. The Yellow Pages will direct you to the right place to find rules and regulations. Explain your intention and regulatory agencies will generally send you everything you should know, free. They are fair, friendly, and will tell you exactly what is needed to operate a business. Don't get buffaloed on this part. It is easy (a 10-year-old can handle reports), and the cost to you generally is little or nothing. "Acting dumb" to see what might happen seldom pays.

Check with your insurance company. The "personal liability" coverages you have now may also cover you and your little business, but check it out. Insurance companies don't cover workmen or workmanship, only liability. If you fall through a window or rip a couch while washing the ceiling, you are covered under the liability section. However, if you break the window or rip the couch while working on it, you are responsible. Do arm yourself with the necessary insurance, but don't get caught up in morbid fears of what might happen. You'll have a few bad experiences, but be careful and conscientious and your victims will have great compassion, unless you splash a big drop of ammonia in the eye of a Rembrandt.

4. **Advertise.** A business card pinned up in a laundromat or on a supermarket bulletin board will never get you the kind of people you want to work for. If they can't afford or don't have a washing machine, they generally won't be needing or affording you. Classified ads in the newspaper are always good. Dropping cards off at local businesses gets both owners and clients. But the best advertising for housecleaning is unquestionably the personal referral. Women who have their homes cleaned professionally love to brag about it, and if you do a good job, you'll never be able to handle the work that will flow in. A card or

VARSITY CONTRACTORS, INC.
Residential and Commercial

232-8600

Don A. Aslett, Owner
253 East Halliday

Reminder: Use Varsity for your summer painting needs!

Spring Clean-up Specials

Let Varsity Bring Spring to You!
- **Window Washing**
- **Floor Stripping**
- **Wall Washing**
- **One Time Clean-ups**
- **Carpet Shampooing**
- **Insurance Specialist**
- **Painting**

SNAP

two left at a house or a business will quickly find its way into the hands of a friend, and you'll find your way into another assignment. If your work is good (even if it is a little expensive), your business will boom and prosper.

5. **Start small, and test it out.** You'll be surprised what happens. One thing it will do is make your own housework easier and simpler.

6. Some of the best sources for work (and reliable payment) are:
- Local personal residence cleaning.
- Smoke-loss cleaning jobs for insurance companies.
- Small medical or professional offices.
- Construction cleanup, such as in new housing developments. (Be sure to get your money quick.)

7. Some accounts to avoid:
- People moving out and away.
- Shopping malls and supermarkets.
- "Maid" work for finicky old ladies.

8. **Hire cautiously.** Wrapped up in the thrill and vanity of becoming a "big boss," there is a tendency to promise every ambitious or down-and-out friend a job. Be careful. You could end up working for *them* at no pay. Once some of your friends, relatives or other job-needing associates go on a job with you, you will feel obligated to keep and use them on every job, even if they turn out to be worthless. You'll end up spending all of your time assigning, supervising, and cleaning up after them. Go slow. Start with yourself and a reliable helper (an immediate family member), and work up from there.

9. **Get your own equipment.** You wouldn't be very impressed if a high-class restaurant asked you to bring your own dishes, or a surgeon asked you to furnish the scalpel.

There is power and mystery in "professional equipment and supplies." They are dependable, deductible, and usable in your own home. Don't go over your head on expensive specialty items if your business doesn't justify it. The equipment list in Chapter 2 should give you a good start. Put your name and emblem on all your equipment, for security and advertisement. You don't need a great deal of equipment, and you can store it in the garage and transport it in your car. If your business expands and you need a bigger vehicle, get a van. You don't need a fur-lined $12,800 van. A late-model one is great because you won't be driving it that much—maybe a couple of miles, and then it's parked for hours while you clean a house. There is no sense carrying the insurance, interest, and overhead on an expensive new one. You'll probably only put 5,000 miles or less a year on the vehicle as most of your work will be close to you. Paint your van white or a bright color and letter it. It will be great advertising for you. Don't let your husband use it to go fishing or haul firewood or let the teenagers use it for a "cool" car. Have a few simple shelves built into it, and install curtains if there are any windows. The curtains will serve two purposes: they make the van look more homey, and they reduce temptation to thieves.

10. **Involve the family.** These days there aren't enough paper routes or grocery store box-boy jobs to go around. Once you get a client and she loves and trusts you, she will need other services such as painting, grass cutting, and yard work. This is a natural for your children while you clean the house. Imagine your husband cleaning the fireplace or toilet bowl under your strict supervision. (It will probably never happen, but it's a great thought anyway.)

11. **Fill your work list and time schedule.** Having a small housecleaning

business is not going to give you an ulcer. Booking your own clients leaves you the master. You have the freedom to work just a couple of hours a week—or 80, if you have the energy. Every woman's family and social obligations are as unique as her physical stamina and emotional needs. If all your children are in school, then you will have three hours in the morning and three hours in the afternoon. You could work all week or once a week. Many businesses like their cleaning work done from 4:00 to 6:00 a.m., and if you are a nervous-energy type like me, that is a good time. You are the captain of your own ship; you decide when, where and how. If you can't conform to a client's wishes, or bend enough

to meet them, don't bother with them. They can get someone else. The reason you got into the business was to run it your way, not to let it run you.

Job Sheet Record

Name _____ Phone _____

Address _____ Bus. Phone _____

Insurance Company _____ Phone _____

Address _____ Adjuster _____

Job scheduled for   19   A.M.   P.M.

ROOMS	CLEANING			PAINTING				RUGS	MISCELLANEOUS		
	Wall	Ceil.	W.W.	Wall	Ceil.	W.W.	Color #		Windows	Floors	Amount
Living											
Dining											
Kitchen											
Hall											
Bed											
Bed											
Bed											
Landing											
Entrance											
Recreation											
Utility											
Bath											
Bath											
Basement											
Den											

1. All cleaning of walls—ceiling—woodwork$		Cost $	Cost $	Cost $	Cost $
2. All cleaning of carpets and rugs	$				
3. All cleaning of floors and tile	$		Upholstery		
4. All cleaning of contents—articles	$				
5. All cleaning of upholstery	$		Couch		
6. All cost of drape-cleaning & hanging	$		Couch		
7. Cost of windows	$		Chair		
8. Cost of repair or replacement	$		Chair		
9. Total cost of painting	$		Chair		
10.	$				
11.	$				
TOTAL COST OF BILL	$				

This proposal includes all costs of equipment, supplies, labor and other expenses needed to complete the job as outlined above. Any additional services performed over and above that which is outlined will be considered extra work and will result in additional cost. Your acceptance of this proposal as set forth herein will be indicated by your directing us to commence with the work described herein. We shall be paid the sum of '_____ for the work outlined herein. Work will be completed before any payment is made and work will be done wholly at our risk.

Authorized Signature _____

W-Wash   D-Dry Sponge   S-Shampoo   SW-Scrub & Wax   P-Paint

Maintenance Service Agreement

THIS AGREEMENT entered into on _____ between

_____ hereinafter referred to as "company" and VARSITY CONTRACTORS, INC., hereinafter referred to as "contractor." Service address:

Contractors will furnish for the company building maintenance, supplies and services as outlined in the attached "Detailed Contract Work Schedule" which is made a part hereof by reference, in accordance with the conditions and specifications set forth in this agreement for a period of _____ months beginning _____, 19____. At the end of twelve months of each year of anniversary date the agreement will be renewed following the negotiable review of specifications and terms of the agreement between company and contractor.

In consideration of the above, the company agrees to pay to the contractor $_____ per month for outlined service plus other costs for additional services as agreed upon. Said sum shall be due and payable TEN DAYS after each of the preceding month's services have been rendered.

TERMS: It is mutually agreed that:

1. All work shall be performed by the contractor in a good and workmanlike manner, and the contractor shall also provide regular inspections by the contractor's supervisory personnel of all premises on which the services are provided to assure a high quality of work by contractor of services agreed upon in the Detailed Contract Work Schedule.

2. All persons employed by the contractor in the performance of services hereunder shall be under the sole and exclusive direction and control of the contractor.

3. All property brought onto the premises by contractor is owned by contractor and not subject to any lien or encumbrance resulting from any action of the company. The contractor may remove such property during any normal business hour at contractor's convenience without prejudice.

4. Contractor agrees to carry Contractor Liability Insurance for personal and property damage at the amounts required. Certificates of such insurance issued by the insuring carrier(s) shall be furnished upon request to the company. Contractor agrees to comply with the local compensation insurance regulations and to provide and pay all employee federal, state, and municipal taxes including, but not limited to, Social Security, unemployment, federal and state withholding and other taxes.

5. Company agrees to pay ONE AND ONE-HALF PERCENT (1½%) per month interest (18% annual percentage rate) charge on any past due accounts and agrees to pay any costs including reasonable attorney fees to enforce the provisions of this agreement.

122

6. Company agrees to hold the contractor harmless for any property damage claims in excess of $50,000.

7. In case of default by the company under this agreement, the contractor may proceed to collect amounts owing and/or take possession of all contractor-owned equipment.

8. In the event that the contractor continues to provide services on this contract beyond the initial term of this agreement and/or in the event of proceeding in bankruptcy against either of the parties, or if either party elects to terminate for any reason whatsoever, it is agreed that this contract will continue in effect until THIRTY DAYS after written notice of termination is given by either party. Notice is to be given in writing with proof of delivery.

9. Modification of this agreement may be made by mutual consent of the parties, which must be done in writing and attached hereto, dated and signed.

10. Company may, at its option, request the contractor to perform additional services beyond those listed on the attached detailed Contract Work Schedule. However, company agrees that any additional or extra work will be performed as per price specified at time of performance and in accordance with the terms of this agreement.

11. Company may not assign its right to this agreement without written consent from contractor.

12. Unless exempt under the rules and regulations of the Secretary of Labor or other proper authority, this contract is subject to applicable laws and executive orders relating to equal opportunity and nondiscrimination in employment. The parties hereto shall not discriminate in their employment practices against any person by reason of race, creed, color, sex or national origin and agree to comply with the provisions of said laws and orders to the extent applicable in the performance of work or furnishing of services, materials or supplies hereunder. No services will be performed which in contractor's opinion pose a safety hazard to contractor's employees.

13. It is the express intention of the parties that this agreement, its status, or form is at all times in the county of_____, state of _____ , in which county and state all matters whether in contract or tort relating to the validity, construction, interpretation, and enforcement of this contract shall be determined.

Additional terms:

Acceptance:

_____	_____	_____
Date	Agent for Company	Title

_____	_____	_____
Date	Agent for Varsity Contractors, Inc.	Title

_____
Property Owner, if not same as Agent

18

Your Reward: There Is Life After Housework

Well, that's it. We've covered enough aspects of housework to provide a fresher, more realistic view of the subject. And until a robot is developed that can be programmed to do your housework for you, you'll find the methods and equipment outlined in the foregoing 17 chapters to be the next best thing for getting the most work done in the least amount of time.

Personal freedom is life's real reward. Housework is an important and worthy endeavor, but the less of your life it requires, the more will be available for the other pursuits that add dimension and joy and meaning to living. As I've already stated, housework may be your responsibility, but it is not your destiny. Your real role in the home goes far beyond housework.

What you used to see as the thankless chores of housework might well be some of your greatest teaching moments . . . time to help the family and yourself develop an improved attitude and new respect for this important aspect of living.

Think "teaching moment" the next time . . . you spend four hours preparing a lovely family dinner and get only a three-foot stack of dirty dishes . . . your 16 hours spent sewing a satin drill team costume are rewarded with a whimper about the hemline . . . you proudly present a fat, tidy row of freshly ironed white shirts and he says "Where's my blue one?" . . . you're on duty around the clock nursing the family through a siege of the flu, yet when it's your turn to collapse into a sickbed, there's not a soul around to nurse you . . . you know the kids are home by the trail of coats and books left in their wake . . . or by the jam and peanut butter and empty glasses covering the counter.

Remember, if *you* don't teach them, who will?

Don't come unglued if you sometimes discover that even after applying all the best methods of housecleaning and management, you nevertheless experience some of the mundane realities of the profession. Every job has them, and housework is no exception. So brace yourself, and take it with a smile, for you too are vulnerable to slipping vacuum belts, flyspecked windows, plugged sink drains, sticky kitchen floors, ring around the collar, muddy boots, tidal waves of dirty laundry, and five dozen cookies to bake for the Halloween party (on two hours' notice).

But you've made tremendous progress! You've learned the basic mechanics of effective housecleaning, and you've become more aware of the true nature of a homemaker's role. You've also seen the error of the notion that anything to do with cleaning and housework is unglamorous and unrewarding.

I've been exposed to the same image you have of "the unglamorous job of cleaning," and I am still confronted with it every day. As I mentioned earlier, I ran my business while going to college. I received several newspaper write-ups and a lot of publicity,

and everyone figured my cleaning activities were great as well as being different—*as long as they were leading to something else.* When I finished my schooling and still remained a cleaner, my social prestige diminished greatly. Several little things, most of them unquestionably humorous, brought this to my attention.

I was doing a special job in the bank, cleaning the vault floors with a buffer. Customers were still drifting in and out of the bank, casting pitying glances, as they usually do, at the "janitor." I was involved in community affairs, had five children, was a scout leader, active churchman, went to the symphony, and thought I was riding the tide of social prestige along with the rest of upstanding society. One of the bank's customers, an irritable lady, was dragging her loud and disobedient child along when suddenly in disgust she grabbed the little fellow, shook him violently, and, gesturing toward me, said, "Behave, you little snot, or you'll end up just like him!"

As the days progressed, I found that her opinion of cleaning people was nearly universal. Whenever I'm mingling in a new group and my accomplishments are described, a newcomer will always ask, "Well, what does he do for a living?" Every time there follows a hesitation and silence. Nobody wants to say, "He's a cleaning man." People who meet me on the street and remember me from the early days because of the publicity my housecleaning business received will inevitably ask, "Well, how are you, Don? What are you doing now? Are you still a. . . ." They always hesitate because they can't say "housecleaner."

While at college, my daughter Laura skiied at the nearby resorts whenever she and her friends got the chance. Since she had the car that could haul the most skis and students, it was generally used as a taxi. After everyone was loaded in and they were off to the mountain, someone in all the jabbering would always comment, "This is sure a nice car. What does your dad do for a living?" My daughter, who has enjoyed the status of "cleaner" since the age of 12, always answered cheerfully, "He's a janitor." The interior of the car would go silent for approximately three minutes, no one knowing what to say. Finally, in a meek, polite voice, someone would patronizingly say, "That's nice."

One of my managers, right after he was listed in *Who's Who in Technology Today in the U.S.A.,* was registering his wife at the hospital to have a baby. When the clerk asked the manager his occupation, he answered confidently, "Janitor." She looked up at him and said shyly, "Oh, come on now. You don't really want me to put that down, do you?"

I could relate dozens of such stories, all hinging on the questionable status of being a "cleaning person." The image and status that society associates with cleaning—in business or the home—is totally incorrect. I recently taught my traveling housecleaning seminar for a dental group. When someone asked how toilet cleaning related to dentists, I informed them, "We both work in enamel, don't we?" Voting in a Senate chamber is no more important than cleaning a bed chamber! A glittering restaurant has no more vital things take place in it than your ordinary, everyday kitchen. Those who have immersed themselves in the business enjoy it—find it an exhilarating life. The home is the most sacred and exciting place on the face of the earth. And *you* control it and have the responsibility of keeping it in order.

Women are forever targets for the misguided notion that in order to build up the image and credibility of women in the business world, the work and image of women in the home must be discredited and destroyed. Don't buy it! For a woman to pronounce that caring for her own home is a hardship, a drag, and a bore is only to admit a lack of imagination and creativity. Those who clean and care for a house, whether on a full-time basis or in addition to another career, can enjoy it tremendously.

Houses are more than showcases and status symbols. Your house is your home—the background against which your life is lived. Why direct all your efforts toward impressing society? There's fun and great satisfaction in the giving of yourself to your surroundings, and in making your home a pleasing and interesting reflection of your personality. People will enjoy coming to your house, not because of its impressive trappings and expensive adornments, but because so much of YOU is there. All homes should radiate the particular tastes, interests and attitudes of the family who lives there.

Maintaining a high standard of cleanliness is very important, but it should never become *all*-important. There is great virtue in being meticulous, in adding that extra touch of excellence to your efforts. But there is also room for caution here: In our zeal to achieve superior results in our work, we sometimes reach a point beyond which our performance can become slavish devotion to meaningless detail. The use of our time can, at this point, be downright inefficient and ineffective. We want to put "first things first." Living is life . . . and we want to have as much of it as possible after housework!

It's essential to spend plenty of time with the kids. But children, and grown-ups too, need order in their lives. A feeling of contentment and well-being grows out of neatness and order rather than clutter and chaos. High self-esteem and achievement germinate in a quality environment, and no environment is more influential than the home. The atmosphere and condition of our homes have a great deal of influence on all of us. They have more power to affect lives than do movie stars, presidents, or professors. The spirit of your home can touch and change not only the lives of all those who enter and all who live there, but it will also have an influence on your

intimate personal relationships and your love for other people. Much of that enriched life is gained by developing and applying the principles of good organization and intelligent cleaning. These same principles will make you irresistible as a person . . . someone to be needed, loved and appreciated.

It is difficult for us to hide what we are, for our countenances generally betray our feelings. Most of our feelings are projected in the climate and conditions within the home. A woman, regardless of status, family size, age, or any of life's buffetings, will find it all worthwhile if her home is a sane, comfortable, orderly place.

Managing the home is usually a woman's responsibility, not necessarily because she is a woman but because no one else can do it. Some men think they can, but they can't. A woman has a power and influence no man ever will.

If mechanics were all that was involved in housework, a man might well be better for the job than you are. But when it comes to bringing out the charm of a room, or adding the beauty and special warmth that make a clean home more than just a clean house . . . well, that transcends the realm of applied science or mechanics, and I'll admit without reservation . . . that takes a woman!

The good Lord knew what he was doing when he shoved men out into the world to plow the fields, sail the ships, operate the machines, and haggle in the business world. He knew that with a little brawn and some brains, we men could be taught to handle those things.

But the home is where he needed the artists. That is where he needed the concentration of intellect and sensitivity and devotion and creativity. It was the home front that needed the real multifaceted managers and the natural diplomats.

In teaching, marriage counseling, and employing numerous people, I have found

that women are special! In speaking assignments, for example, I've faced every size and type of audience imaginable, but every time I face an audience of women, I feel a great deal of warmth and compassion. It is real and it radiates from women whereas it doesn't from men. Many a philosopher and psychologist has tried to convince me that women are as mean, evil, scheming, and lazy as men, but I'm positive the philosophers are wrong. I grew up in a good home. My sister, my mother, aunts, and two grandmothers were all beautiful, positive people. I was 18 before I ever heard a woman swear. The longer I live, the more apt I am to place women on a pedestal.

It is a delight and a marvel to see what a woman can do with a house. I'm continually in awe of a woman's ability to make things inviting with cheerful decorating ideas, plants and flowers, imaginative color schemes, and all the special little touches that have such a pleasant and positive influence upon our moods and senses.

Pulpit, pedestal, or poetry cannot come as close to enriching the lives of others as can a woman with a good, clean, happy, well-organized, well-disciplined life at home. Humankind needs examples of order and confidence. Both of these virtues can be superbly exemplified by a woman and a home. The home is the power lever of the world, and *you* control it. If you have not or are not now experiencing exhilaration from your role as a homemaker, it is possibly because your family has so much emotional and physical clutter that none of them can reach each other to give love and appreciation. There is no greater goal or achievement on the face of the earth than the opportunity to love and in turn be loved. Thrashing around in the clutter of the home too often thwarts the opportunity to achieve this.

You can change it. Then it will change you. You don't have to ask for love. You have the power to possess it and you will.

THERE IS LIFE AFTER HOUSEWORK!

About the Author

DON A. ASLETT

Don A. Aslett isn't just convinced that there is life after housework: He champions the belief that there is life everywhere every minute, and everyone has a sacred obligation to take full advantage of it. Since his birth in a small southern Idaho town, Don has pursued every channel of opportunity available to him. Teachers wrote on his grade school report cards, "He intensely takes over and never runs out of energy." At age 15 his parents taught and then assigned him to operate 80 acres of the family farm. He was actively involved in high school athletics and school government. When the town, the church, or the county fair needed a fund-raising production, Don—as a high school student—would take over and produce it. He left for college knowing how to work for the other guy, but found it unchallenging and so launched his own business career in cleaning, organizing a group of college students into a professional housecleaning and building maintenance operation called Varsity Contractors.

Don's first love, writing, has never been dormant. Throughout years of building a family, career, and business, he has amassed volumes on a unique variety of subject matter. Just a few years ago, he felt it time to begin to compile, publish, and market what he had written. In 1979, at the request of thousands of homemakers who wanted his seminar information in writing, he wrote *Is There Life After Housework?*.

Today, Don is senior stockholder in a leading maintenance firm and owner of a consulting company whose prime client is the Bell System. He is a popular youth speaker and leader, devoting much of his time to family, church, and scouting. Don has taught hundreds of housecleaning seminars to enthusiastic audiences throughout the United States. He and his wife Barbara and their six children reside on a small ranch in the southern mountains of Idaho.

Index

Floor finish, 13
Floors, 38-39, 53-59; appearance of, 53; cleanability of, 53-54; color of, 59; concrete, 58; hard, 53, 54, 62; no-wax, 55; protection of, 53; "soft," 61-62; wood, 58-59
Floor squeegee, 13, 56, 58, 59
Furniture, 77-80
Furniture polish, 78

G

Grease stains, 40, 89, 98; on furniture, 78

H

Hard-finish fabric, 78-79
Hard floors, 53, 54, 62
Hard-to-reach areas, 81-86
Hard water buildup, 39-40, 103, 105, 106; on windows, 45
Hardwood floors. *See* Hard floors
High places, 81-86, 111
Hole patching, 99
Household cleaners, 40

I

Indoor-outdoor carpet, 62, 111
Installation of carpet, 61
Interlock polymer finish, 13, 57

J

Janitorial supply house, 10, 42, 45, 49, 58, 70, 80, 104
Junk: disposal and dispersal of, 25; origin of, 24-25

L

Ladders, 82-83, 91
Latex paint, 88, 98
Law of 80/20, 95
Law of the Packrat, 24
Law of 70/30, 25
List making, 16, 19-20
Low-luster "velvet clear finish," 98

M

Maintenance, 57; of carpets, 62-63; decorating for, 110; ease of, 110-111; planning of, 110
Masonry cinderblock walls, 98
Matting, 47-51, 54, 59, 62, 64, 65
Membrane finish, 78, 98
Mildew, 106-107
Mineral buildup, 103
Mineral salts, 39
Mineral spirits, 95, 100

Mop bucket, 12, 54, 55, 70
Mops, 12, 39, 54, 56, 57
"Multiple track" organization, 17

N

Natural wood, 78, 94, 95, 98, 111
Neutral cleaners, 13, 57, 58, 90, 94
No-wax floors, 55
Nylon pads, 13, 55-56, 57, 58, 95
Nylon-tuft mats, 49-50
Nylon, vinyl-backed mats, 49-50

O

Oil-base solvents, 40
Organization, 15-22, 128; myths about, 16-18

P

Packrat law, 24
Paint, selection of, 99
Paintbrushes, 98, 99; cleaners for, 100; storage of, 101
Painting, 97-101; and cleaning, 7, 95, 98-99; cleanup after, 100; preparation for, 98-99; techniques for, 99-100
Paint remover, 59
Paint rollers, 98, 99; extension handles for, 99; pans for, 99; removal of paint from, 100
Paint thinner, 40, 93, 95, 100
Paneling, 94
Patching of holes, 99
Petroleum base cleaners, 40
Phosphoric acid cleaner, 45, 103
Planks, 83, 85, 101. *See also* Scaffolding
Plastic spray bottles, 10, 12, 94, 104
Polymer finish, 13, 57
Powdered cleansers, 40. *See also* Abrasive cleansers
Preparation for painting, 98-99
Prevention, 47-51, 103
Preventive maintenance, 105
Primer, 99
Professional carpet shampooing, 67-68
Professional housecleaning business, 113-123
Protection: of floors, 53; of wood, 98
Push-pull type squeegee, 13, 56

R

Rags, 89
Rayon layflat mop, 12, 54
Residues in carpet, 62
Resinous finish on wood floors, 58
Restorability of furniture, 78-79
Roller mop bucket, 12, 70
Rollers. *See* Paint rollers

Roller-type wringer for mop, 12, 54

Want More Information?

Now that you've seen how you can save hours of housework each week, share this housecleaning system with your friends and relatives by ordering extra copies of *Is There Life After Housework?*—a great gift for Mother's Day, Christmas, birthdays, weddings, or any special occasion.

Use these coupons to order *Is There Life After Housework?* and Don Aslett's new book, *Do I Dust or Vacuum First?*, which answers the 100 most-often-asked housecleaning questions!

YES! Please rush me:
QTY.

_____ Is There Life After Housework?, $6.95
_____ Do I Dust or Vacuum First?, $6.95

Send to: **Writer's Digest Books**   9933 Alliance Road
Cincinnati, Ohio 45242

Please add $1.50 postage and handling for one book, 50¢ for each additional book. Ohio residents add 5½% sales tax. Allow 30 days for delivery.

_____ Check or money order enclosed.
_____ Please charge my: ☐ Visa   ☐ MasterCard

Account # _____   Exp. Date _____

Signature _____   Interbank # _____

Name _____
Address _____
City _____   State _____Zip _____
(Prices subject to change without notice)

YES! Please rush me:
QTY.

_____ Is There Life After Housework?, $6.95
_____ Do I Dust or Vacuum First?, $6.95

Send to: **Writer's Digest Books**   9933 Alliance Road
Cincinnati, Ohio 45242

Please add $1.50 postage and handling for one book, 50¢ for each additional book. Ohio residents add 5½% sales tax. Allow 30 days for delivery.

_____ Check or money order enclosed.
_____ Please charge my: ☐ Visa   ☐ MasterCard

Account # _____   Exp. Date _____

Signature _____   Interbank # _____

Name _____
Address _____
City _____   State _____Zip _____
(Prices subject to change without notice)

FOR ADDITIONAL INFORMATION ON:
☐ Where I can get janitorial supplies.
☐ How I can attend a Don Aslett Housecleaning Seminar/Workshop in my area.
☐ How I can sponsor a Don Aslett Housecleaning Seminar/Workshop in my area.
☐ Don Aslett's other publications.

Please write to: Don Aslett
P.O. Box 1682
Pocatello, ID 83204